BOYS IN LITTLE ITALY: A COMPARISON OF THEIR INDIVIDUAL VALUE ORIENTATIONS, FAMILY PATTERNS, AND PEER GROUP ASSOCIATIONS

ALBERT S. ALISSI

San Francisco, California
1978

Published By

R&E Research Associates, Inc.
4843 Mission Street
San Francisco, California 94112

Publishers
Robert D. Reed and Adam S. Eterovich

Library of Congress Card Catalog Number
77-90360

I.S.B.N.
0-88247-495-2

ACKNOWLEDGMENTS

This work was originally stimulated by a Cleveland Foundation grant which made it possible for me to join the Alta House Staff as Director of the Outreach Project. Relationships with many professionals and related workers during my most recent practice cannot be fully recognized here, but I am grateful to have had the opportunity to work with and learn from so many.

My earlier academic training was greatly influenced by the late Dr. Grace Coyle whom I, like so many, admired and respected. In this current undertaking, I can never fully acknowledge my deep appreciation to my advisor, Dr. Arthur Blum, whose direction, guidance, and assurance during some very difficult times helped me immeasurably.

From a personal perspective, interest in this subject was greatly influenced by my own working-class origins as a member of an extended Italian family. I acknowledge therefore my family and relatives for the early impression they made on my life. To my wife, Sarah, and children, Mike and Amy, I am indebted for their patience and understanding.

I wish also to thank Mrs. Rita Gallitto of the Alta House staff for clerical help far beyond the call of duty. And finally, my sincerest thanks go to all those related to the study -- Alta House Board, Staff, and Members; and especially, the Boys in Little Italy.

TABLE OF CONTENTS

LIST OF TABLES

CHAPTER I

THEORETICAL PERSPECTIVES REGARDING
MAJOR VARIABLES

The Problem

The assumption is often made that a neighborhood, when it reflects a particular social class level, can be treated as a relatively homogeneous unit. This study highlights the limitations of this general assumption for social work practice. Current contrasts drawn between lower-class slums, stable working-class neighborhoods, and middle-class suburbs may be useful for comparative purposes; but, these conceptions are sorely inadequate and misleading for understanding the more internal and distinctive qualities of any given neighborhood. The problem here is to examine the degree to which there is heterogeneity within a single social class and ethnic neighborhood. An attempt will be made to demonstrate that what is often viewed as a homogeneous unit is in fact a composite, resulting from the existence and interaction of diverse behavioral forms which reflect various segments of the larger stratification system.

More specifically, this study seeks to demonstrate the existence of distinct subsystems within a working-class, Italian-American neighborhood.[1] In addition to a traditional working-class orientation, there will also be a mobile middle-class orientation as well as an "inconsistent" deviant subsystem.

The experience of the investigator in working with potentially delinquent boys in groups led to the present interest in comparing that group with other groups of neighborhood boys in relation to subsystem identifications. We will attempt to determine to what extent boys with values or behavior styles characteristic of a particular subsystem will come from similar family types and belong to similar peer groups. It is anticipated that the patterns of distribution according to these variables will be particularly relevant in positioning the boys within the neighborhood.

The practical significance of this inquiry rests on the greater refinement it affords the group worker as a result of conceptualizing the neighborhood in terms of interacting social systems. In particular, it provides a more precise tool for understanding the peer group as a dynamic interacting part of the larger social system in which it is found. A major drawback in current conceptions of the small group in its neighborhood setting has been the tendency to over-apply general social-cultural descriptions; however vague and remote they may be, to the group in question. Thus, while internal group processes such as group formation, structural differentiation, value determination, decision-making, etc., are usually expressed in specific terms; factors external to the group are often neglected because they are considered only in a most generalized sense. To say, for example, that there are vestiges of

1

the extended family among Italian-Americans which create a "neighborhood" suspicion of outsiders does not mean that all persons or all groups in the neighborhood will be influenced accordingly. Surely, newcomers may or may not display similar suspicion. The somewhat generalized concept of the Italian extended family cannot be taken to explain all behavior which just seems to be related. Persons and groups have to be more specifically identified relative to this phenomena before it can be convincingly shown that it has any consistent influence on them.

What is lacking, then, is a more definitive picture of how persons are distributed within the various neighborhood subsystems. This study will try to establish this mapping in one neighborhood by comparing boys who come from a presumably homogeneous neighborhood to see how they differ in relation to: 1) their individual values; 2) their family background; and 3) their peer group associations.

Social Stratification

It has been shown that the position we occupy in the social class system is significant in determining and shaping our material destinies, life chances, behavioral styles, values, and attitudes. To assert this generally accepted proposition is not to belittle the role of the individual as an independent being; but rather to demonstrate that he is inextricably a part of the social order. There are, of course, many situational determinants of behavior which are randomly distributed. We are concerned here only with those responses which are systematically conditioned by the nature of the social structure. Although this focus represents only a segment of the total human experience which needs to be considered in the practice of social work, it is most essential for developing a meaningful social perspective on behavior.

Essentially, the study of social stratification[2] is concerned with understanding the patterned differences among people through the analysis of the processes whereby they are ranked and ordered. Although, in general social class pertains to one's hierarchical positions in the social order, the concept of social class differs depending upon the theoretical context in which it is used. Early scholarly interest in the subject was preoccupied with the more objective and material aspects of social class and theories were phrased largely in economic terms. The objective reality of social class behavior was apparent in Marx's concept of the class struggle which was based on the great disparity in wealth between the "haves" and the "have nots."[3] Weber greatly expanded this economic monism as he differentiated class in its economic sense from status and party which were designated as two closely related dimensions of stratification.[4] American interest in the subject generally stressed the more intangible, subjective aspects of social class which were often revealed in attitudes and sentiments. Many empirical studies now exist to demonstrate how virtually every aspect of behavior whether social, economic, political, or religious in nature is subjected to the forces emanated from the stratification system.[5] Much current theoretical interest centers around the so-called functional explanation which maintains that stratification is functionally important and necessary to carry out the major values which society emphasizes.[6]

Of fundamental importance in the functional approach is the concept that social phenomena cannot be studied effectively without corresponding attention to the functional interdependency of social units to each other and to the larger whole. Obviously, this conception goes beyond the study of social stratification. A functional analysis of any set of social circumstances can be a useful tool for deriving fresh hypotheses and developing theory whatever the problem.[7] The functional approach is particularly relevant here to suggest that the values a person holds bear some functional relationship to his family and peer group patterns.

A thorough review of the literature on social stratification will reveal that social class is associated with values, family life, and (to a lesser known degree) peer group associations. Our more limited treatment of these variables will also bear this out. However, in order to understand more fully why these variables may be expected to be related to each other, a variety of theories must be considered. To arrive at a suitable theoretical perspective, we will start with an analysis of social systems with particular reference to the small group.

Social Systems Analysis

Theoretical Perspective

It is central to our view that the more internal aspects of group processes are so much a part of the processes of the larger external community that these two processes can be studied simultaneously and in the same terms. Loomis takes this position in his analysis of social systems. Taking interaction to be the core concept, he notes that in time interaction tends to develop certain uniformities some of which persist. As these become orderly or systematic they are recognized as social systems. Therefore, a social system is simply defined as the patterned interactions of participants.[8]

This concept of social systems directs attention to varying characteristic levels of interaction, and applies whether we are dealing with direct, face-to-face personal interactions in a small group; or, with the indirect, impersonal interaction of any number of larger collectivities in society. The crucial point is that whatever social system is being viewed, "...the elements that constitute it as a social system and the processes that articulate it remain the same."[9] It is then possible to consider any variety of systems or subsystems in the same terms whether they are neighborhoods, families, peer groups or any other recognized entity.

Furthermore, to truly understand a social system it is necessary to know how it is related or not related to other systems. To explicate this, Loomis deals with the processes of systemic linkage and boundary maintenance. A number of common elements are found to exist in all systems which he identifies as belief, sentiment, norm, status-role, rank, power, sanction, and facility. Systemic linkage is the process ". . . whereby one or more of the elements of at least two social systems is articulated in such a manner that the two systems in some ways and on some occasions may be viewed as a single unit."[10] On the other hand, boundary maintenance is defined as the process whereby the identity of the social system is preserved and patterned interactions are maintained. Thus, the concept of systemic linkage implies organizational arrangements for group interdependencies; while boundary maintenance refers to the limits set on inter-group contacts.

Descriptive Typology

This perspective on social systems forms the basis upon which a neighborhood or any of its parts can be analyzed. To the extent that certain individuals, families, and groups are linked together, they can be recognized as a neighborhood subsystem distinguishable from other similarly linked individuals, families, and groups. While the neighborhood in this study has been viewed from the outside as a homogeneous system of relations which are characteristically ethnic, we have observed at least three major subsystems which appear to exist in dynamic interaction. These are developmental in the sense that they provide "designs for living" in the form of norms, values, and behavior patterns for their members from childhood through adulthood. Depending upon the degree to which persons become carriers of these patterns, they will have established places in the subsystem. The three subsystems for purposes of this study are designated as traditional, mobile, or deviant.

The traditional subsystem:--This subsystem is composed of individuals, families, and groups who are affected most strongly by neighborhood traditions and values generally characteristic of close-knit, Italian communities such as "Little Italy". Its members are well organized and share a strong sense of solidarity based on mutual, informal obligations. Law and its enforcement mechanisms in general are not to be trusted for there is a preference for handling neighborhood affairs internally within a network of strong, informal controls.[11] Persons who live by this rather strictly enforced code of behavior feel that they "belong" and can rely on the active support of others in the subsystem. The close-knit character of relationships tends to keep members isolated from the wider community although workable relations are maintained with such community agencies as the church, school, and settlement.

The mobile subsystem:--This subsystem is made up of persons who aspire to achieve or have achieved a greater measure of personal resources, and who take advantage of wider community opportunities which lead to increased education, better jobs, and broader interests. While in a sense they belong and are part of the neighborhood, and can rely on help and backing from the traditional subsystem, they can usually do without this help because they are independently sufficient and resourceful in establishing meaningful contacts with the outside community. Members do not share as intimately in the mutual obligations and expectations of the organized code of behavior so characteristic of the traditional subsystem. The mobile person is characterized by his ability to act somewhat independently and adopt new forms of behavior as the need arises. Adult members of this subsystem tend to take on leadership roles in neighborhood institutions which are part of the wider community network such as the church, the P.T.A., the settlement, and the like.[12]

The deviant subsystem:--Those who make up the deviant subsystem are most often viewed by other neighborhood residents and institutional representatives as troublemakers, isolates, or non-conformists. The major tendency of these persons is to incur negative societal reactions[13] from other residents. A variety of persons are found to be members of this deviant subsystem--the southern white newcomers, foreign-born Italians, resident students, the criminal element, or long-time residents who for one reason or another fail to live up to the behavioral requirements of the other two subsystems. There are differences and inconsistencies within this group. Entire families may have lower status in the neighborhood, completely lacking in any social acceptance whatsoever. On the

4

other hand, criminals enjoy a mixed status, having resources and power, but lacking respectability. Their status appears to be related to the fear they generate in others. By and large, all members of the subsystem are influenced by the prevalent neighborhood code, but their behavior appears to vary instrumentally to deal with their marginal position. Most often their behavioral style is characterized as being disruptive, troublesome, or simply alien to the mainstream of neighborhood life.

As these descriptions indicate, differences exist within the neighborhood which reflect the range of functioning found in the wider community. However, it is true that there are common values and behavioral expectations which together present the impression of one unified and distinct subculture.[14] For example, all boys to some degree show ethnic and neighborhood identifications based on similar backgrounds and current living conditions. Other similarities are reflected in commonly held prejudices towards outsiders, especially Negroes, adherence to certain neighborhood codes, and a common identification as one of the "neighborhood boys."

To understand any particular group, however, it must be analyzed in relation to other social systems which have some bearing on its functioning. Thus, in the positioning of one group, other groups must, by necessity, be considered as the entire configuration of group types is in effect chartered.[15] Starting with a discussion of the potential delinquent and delinquent boys group, we will proceed to examine it as a group type in contrast to other group types which are found in the neighborhood subsystems. But the analysis cannot stop there. In addition to group types, the subsystem distinctions also differentiate individual values and basic family types. We will consider each of these independently although it is understood that these variables are in practice intertwined.

Group Association

Theoretical Perspective

The full-fledged delinquent gang has been defined as ". . . one in which certain forms of delinquent activity are essential requirements for the performance of the dominant roles supported by the subculture."[16] This conception is somewhat limited in applicability. To say, for example, that most delinquency occurs among groups does not necessarily mean that the groups are of the full-fledged delinquent variety. Experience has shown that while there are such groups, much delinquent behavior occurs only among small cliques within larger groups consisting of two or three individuals and does not involve the total group membership.[17]

Furthermore, the potential delinquent group does not necessarily qualify as a full-fledged delinquent gang. We must ask certain questions concerning the make-up of the potential delinquent group: Whom does it attract? What function does the group serve for its members? What functions does it serve with respect to other groups and the larger social system within which it is found? The use of the term "potential"[18] is used here to distinguish it from the confirmed delinquent. Theory has not taken into account the various group types in a developmental sense. There are critical differences between the adolescent delinquent gang and the early pre-adolescent group that takes on an appearance of

5

a gang during one stage of its development. They occupy different positions in the life cycle and have different kinds of problems.

It has been only recently that sociologists have undertaken the task of theorizing with respect to the emergence of the delinquent subculture and examining the conditions under which persons become carriers of this subculture. Cohen[19] provided a new way of thinking about the relationship between the class norms of American society and the anti-social gang as a culture subform. He states that the delinquent subculture arises out of the socially structured gap between the aspirations of the lower-class boys and the means realistically available to them to meet the requirements of the middle-class dominated institutions. As a result, they suffer status deprivation and low self-esteem. The presence of a large number of such boys in "effective interaction" in urban areas leads to the development of a set of group-held values which serves as an effective solution to problems of working-class boys in conflict with middle-class norms.

Actually, three possible responses to "the adjustment problem" are seen to be possible. One alternative is to desert the traditional working-class orientation and accept the challenge of the middle-class status system. This has been termed a College-boy[20] response as its life style is patterned after middle-class behavior. A second alternative is to accept a "stable corner-boy response" which is characterized by its intimate participation in a close-knit primary group militating against upward mobility. This response makes it possible to maintain good working relations with the working-class way of life. A third alternative is the adoption of a genuine delinquent response. Whereas the corner-boys "temporize" with middle-class morality, the full-fledged delinquent subculture repudiates it and sets up its own values for behavior.[21]

Cohen describes the content of the delinquent subculture as non-utilitarian, malicious, and negativistic; and is characterized by what he calls "short-run hedonism" and "group autonomy." This is furthermore interpreted to be an ". . . explicit and wholesale repudiation of middle-class standards and the adoption of their very antithesis."[22]

Cloward and Ohlin evolved a theory of differential opportunity structures. In their view, any individual's position in the social system can be viewed relative to the availability of legal and illegal opportunities. Given limited access to success goals by legitimate means, the delinquent response varies according to the degree to which illegitimate opportunities prevail. Three distinct types of delinquent subcultures are described as criminal, conflict, and retreatist. The criminal is devoted to theft and other illegal means of securing income. This type most often arises where there is an integration of older and younger offenders which provides a kind of "racket" opportunity structure. The conflict type of subculture arises in disorganized slum areas where there is no integration between the various age levels of offenders. Limited conventional and criminal opportunities along with weak social controls generally favor hostility and fighting. The retreatist subculture is characterized by the use of drugs. Persons experiencing a kind of "double failure" in both legitimate and illegitimate pursuits are likely to retreat into this extreme form of behavior.[23]

W. B. Miller does not view the emergence of the delinquent subculture as a reaction to middle-class norms. Instead he sees it as having distinctive values of its own which derive directly from socialization into the lower-class culture. These values are transmitted by parents and are not reactions to middle-class cultural patterns and status criteria. The focal concerns of the lower-class culture, he states, are trouble, toughness, smartness, excitement, fate, and autonomy. The preoccupation of lower-class persons with these major themes is likely to lead to delinquent activity.[24]

Although these theories tend to support the contention that the emergence of the delinquent subculture is intimately related to its social circumstances,[25] the natural history or developmental aspects remain obscure.[26] The adolescent group responses as outlined represent solutions to respective problems of adjustment. Since less mature persons have presumably not yet reached the point where such alternative decisions are made, their groups represent antecedent forms which are often overlooked in modern theoretical formulations. In this sense, then, among the middle class oriented can be found potential college-boy groups and college-boy groups; among the traditional stable working class can be found potential corner-boy groups and corner-boy groups; and among the deviant can be found the potential delinquent-boy groups and the delinquent-boy groups.[27]

The potential delinquent group can be viewed, therefore, in terms of its systemic linkage within the deviant system. Its age status position relative to other groups in the system and the fact that it is a part of the system will have significance for its relationship to other groups. Since the potential delinquent group has not yet worked out an "effective delinquent solution," unlike the full-fledged delinquent gang, there is still considerable ambiguity in the status positions of the members relative to other persons.[28]

Let us now turn to a closer examination of small groups in order to arrive at a clearer understanding of why certain group properties may be adopted by a particular group. Although the internal aspects of the small group have been studied extensively, very little has been done empirically to see how the various group properties are influenced culturally or how they are related to class differences. It is generally recognized that social class tends to provide a common value orientation among group members, which tends to confine contacts and interaction within the same class. However, the "gross effects of class differences on behavior are seldom apparent in small group research . . ."[29]

We are concerned here with the literature regarding group properties which appear to differentiate groups relative to their social positioning in the neighborhood. The main drawback in this regard is that a suitable typology or classification of group types is not to be found. Consequently, the problem continues to be ". . .that of identifying the theoretically strategic group properties which serve systematically to discriminate the operation of each resultant type of group from the others."[30] Drawing from sociological writings, Merton presents a provisional list of theoretically significant properties of group structure.[31] Four in particular appear to differentiate boys groups as they have been observed in practice. These are: 1) group size; 2) open or closed membership patterns; 3) degree to which members are engaged in the group; and 4) group cohesiveness.

The size of a group is not as easily determined as it would seem for no sharp distinctions can be made between large and small groups.[32]

Simmel's early study of groups and the effect of size on interaction demonstrated that the size of the group invariably determines the forms of social relations that occur.[33] Thus, to the extent that group size facilitates or discourages interaction it can be viewed as a group property affecting a variety of phenomena.

Briefly considered, there is evidence to show that smaller groups allow for greater satisfaction than do larger groups.[34] The frequency, duration, and intimacy of contacts among members are found to decrease as the size of the group increases.[35] Smaller groups tend to maintain a greater unity as a group.[36] Although larger groups have greater resources for problem-solving activity, there is a point of diminishing returns as communication and consensus are more difficult to achieve.[37]

The degree to which membership in a group is open or closed is another property which distinguishes groups. Noting that groups vary in this regard, Simmel observed how elites preferred to remain small and closed; while, political parties and religious bodies more often sought an enlarged and open membership. It is recognized that this open or closed characteristic along with its corresponding effects on group size are significant in order that distinctive social relations be maintained.[38]

This property has been linked to other phenomena as well. Merton, for example, in his treatment of reference group theory relates the open or closed nature of groups to mobility. In his view, nonmembership groups are more likely to be adopted as reference groups in social systems with high rates of social mobility. Thus, where a person is likely to be rewarded by future inclusion in a group (i.e. an open group) he is more likely to adopt it as a reference group as a kind of anticipatory orientation.[39]

Other associative factors are revealed in the following statement which is representative of a generally shared viewpoint: A tightly knit group significantly means both a difficult-to-enter group and one whose members closely identify with each other. The less permeable the group the more value is attached to membership and, in turn, the more intense the adherence to group perspectives.[40]

There is, of course, another entirely different aspect to the question of open versus closed groups. One may concentrate on why individuals choose to be members of groups. Factors affecting voluntary membership or selective entry into groups have been studied extensively.[41] Generally it is recognized that there is a relationship between social class and membership rates--middle-class individuals having higher membership rates than working-class individuals.[42] Geographical and physical proximity have also been emphasized as significant determinants by some writers.[43]

A third group property, namely the degree to which members are engaged in the group, refers to the scope and intensity of the involvement expected or required from group members. At one extreme are those "totalitarian" groups that involve members and regulate their participation completely; while at the other extreme are those "segmented" groups that involve members in very limited ways. The distinctions between primary and secondary, psychegroup and sociogroup, or gemeinschaft and gesellschaft refer to a similar differential involvement or engagement of group members.

The degree to which a group engages its members is not clearly specified in empirical studies[44] but is more often considered as it blends with other group properties. Generally, the greater impact on the primary group on its members is recognized, for the greater the culturally defined degree of engagement in a group, the greater the likelihood that it will act as a reference group shaping values and behavior.[45] The primary group has been found to be particularly significant throughout the life cycle of the working-class person although membership in such groups is not necessarily functional.[46] While gangs are often viewed as totalitarian groups in the literature, recent studies have shown a lesser involvement of members. In fact the gang has been described as an "expressive social movement" lacking the degree of commitment and involvement usually associated with the delinquent subculture.[47]

The degree of involvement in a group may also be viewed in terms of variations among individuals in the same group. Thus some members may be more central to the group and its activities, while others may be nominal or peripheral. Obviously, the stance which is taken in this respect will have functional significance for the entire group. For example, central persons are more likely to influence and be influenced by others, while peripheral persons will be freer to participate in more fleeting ways.[48]

Perhaps no other property has been treated more extensively than cohesion. It is surprising, however, to find that the concept is variously defined and continues to lack empirical precision.[49] Literally it means "to stick together" and is most often understood as such. However the concept may be operationally defined, it is true that no single index is available to measure the sponge-like, pervasive character of cohesion. In fact, it has been shown that differing single measures of cohesion were not necessarily correlated.[50] It has also been shown that the effects or consequences of cohesion may be similar although the sources of such cohesion differ greatly.[51] Newcomb concludes, ". . . the group property of cohesiveness is most useful as a conceptual framework bringing together various properties that are less inclusive, rather than as a single property that can be directly and validly measured."[52]

In the main the findings suggest that high cohesive groups tend to exert more influence on their members than low cohesive groups. There is also a greater degree of member satisfaction in such groups. Therefore, to the extent that the group is able to meet the needs of its members and fulfills certain needed functions it tends to cohere. It also has been noted that high cohesive groups have more extensive group norms and standards resulting in greater uniformity.[53]

It can be said in concluding this section that many studies in the field of small group research have not been considered although the essence of what is known has been discussed. While we have many laboratory studies, the study of groups in their natural setting has been limited. Of special importance in this regard is the need for research which studies groups as part of an interacting system and in continuing relationship to other groups and phenomena in the social environment.

Descriptive Typology

In light of our discussion, three distinct types of groups will be defined for this study, corner boy, college-boy, and deviant-boy groups.

These types are defined here not by their composition,[54] but by the presence or absence of the four group properties which have been discussed—namely, size, open or closed membership, degree of engagement of members and group cohesion.

If, as we have suggested, the potential delinquent group functions for its members as a medium for groping towards an effective solution to problems of adjustment, we can expect it to reveal certain group properties. For example, in its more functional sense, such a group should be relatively large and open. In this way it would permit more new members to come into the group and "try it out" as a possible solution. Similarly, it would be more tolerant of variance and deviancy, and would make fewer demands for engagement upon its members. Thus, the open, less demanding, less cohesive character of the potential delinquent group would be more suited to accommodating a variety of members in their search for status problem solutions. Deviant individuals instrumentally utilize such groups which are more adaptable to their needs.

On the other hand, a view of the corner-boy group should reveal another set of properties. Its high status position in the youth culture is best protected by a smaller, closed group requiring allegiance and almost total engagement. The cohesive, close-knit character of the group is therefore functional for the group.[55]

The college-boy group, in turn, would be expected to be large, relatively open (in comparison to the corner-boy group), less totalitarian, and less cohesive. The basis for such predictions rests in the fact that the activities and interests of the "middle classized" adolescent are consistent with larger societal values. Outside interests and planned group activity, engaged in with design and purpose, would be more in keeping with this orientation. In this sense then, the use of the term college-boy would differ from that which is generally employed.[56] In addition to breaking away from corner-boy influences, the college-boy receives the support and backing from other similarly inclined individuals who, in combination, we have chosen to call the mobile system.

Moreover, it would appear that the college-boy group is especially suited for task-oriented activity usually under school or adult sponsorship. Organized team and individual sports are good examples. While the properties of the corner-boy group help to sustain its position in the working-class youth culture and support its remaining aloof and impervious to outside intervention; the college-boy group adheres to middle-class prescriptions. It is adaptable to acquiring skills not only around tasks to be learned, but also with respect to social intercourse and the development of satisfactory group ways of doing things.

In summary then, we have defined group types according to the degree to which they exhibit certain group properties. The corner-boy group is relatively small in size of membership, closed to outsiders, engages its members totally, and is cohesive. The college-boy group is relatively large, open to outsiders, engages its members in segmented ways, and is less cohesive. The potential delinquent-boy group is viewed here as taking ambiguous forms. It is best defined as being inconsistent in respect to the aforementioned properties and, consequently it may for instrumental reasons resemble the other types at any given point in time. Generally though, a "functional guess" will show this

10

type group to be larger, to be more open in membership, to engage its members in segmented ways, and to be less cohesive.

Individual Values

Theoretical Perspective

Values are tremendously complex and cannot easily be separated from the social and cultural systems of which they are a part. To better understand how values become active determinants of behavior, it seems useful to distinguish between the specific content of the values involved and the systemic context in which they are found. When we consider value content we note the particular choice or interest involved--what is said or felt with respect to good or bad, right or wrong, desirable or undesirable. But when we consider the ways in which values are patterned or structured, we examine how they arise, are shaped and are transmitted. In this sense, then, values are defined relative to some larger functional meaning.[57]

Our treatment of value content will be limited to a few dimensions upon which values are known to vary by social class. We will consider differences in levels of aspiration, types of relationships which are established, and valuations concerning the use of time.

A most significant value theme which has been extensively studied centers around aspirations and achievement. The findings generally show that there is greater striving for success among the middle and upper classes than among the lower classes. In his extensive analysis, Hyman concludes ". . . there is reduced striving for success among the lower classes, an awareness of lack of opportunity, and a lack of valuation of education, normally the major avenue to achievement of high status."[58] Knupfer,[59] in her portrait of the underdog shows how being psychologically underprivileged is reflected in habits of submission, reduced access to information, and lack of verbal facility, and is closely linked to being economically underprivileged. The attendant lower levels of aspiration may in some cases be a sign of apathy and ingrained acceptance of defeat. Sewell, Haller, and Strauss[60] found reduced striving for educational and occupational goals among high school students from lower-class families, even among those with superior intelligence.

Writers using somewhat different terms have stressed the fact that the lower classes are concerned mainly with "getting-by" rather than "getting-ahead." In Cohen and Hodges[61] view, the plight of the lower-class individual is an unhappy one which is only partly determined by objective insecurity and powerlessness. His life style becomes adaptive to his status position and he continues to expect and act in such ways as to continue his underdog status. Miller and Riessman[62] emphasize the striving of the working-class person for stability and security. According to them, many practices such as mutual aid and cooperation are important "adjustive" mechanisms. Getting-by, rather than getting-ahead in middle-class terms of status and prestige, becomes a dominant value among the lower working class.

There is evidence to support the belief that middle-class individuals possess a compelling desire to get ahead. Rosen[63] found that middle-class boys had achievement motivations which were significantly

11

higher than those found among lower-class boys. The study also revealed a significant relationship between achievement motivation and grades, and between values and educational aspirations. In another study, it was found that social class was more significant than ethnicity with respect to achievement motivation.[64]

It has not been clearly established, however, that it is simply a matter of reduced striving among members of the lower class. Many writers believe that lower-class individuals have internalized the "getting-ahead" tradition so characteristic of the society as a whole. Indeed this notion is central to Merton's means/end distinction between culturally prescribed aspirations and the socially structured channels for realizing the aspirations.[65] Gould maintains that the lower classes may in fact be more strongly motivated to achieve than those in the higher strata. This is based on the theory that one's concept of the future is seen in terms of the present and lower-class persons are imbedded with a "deep all-pervading need to leave the present."[66]

It is generally accepted that most children in American society, regardless of class of origin, assimilate to some degree the middle-class value system typical of the society as a whole. This does not mean, however, that all of the social classes accept this cultural emphasis to the same degree. While these differences are greatly influenced by a variety of factors, the evidence seems to support the assumption that striving for success is more poignant and pervasive among the middle class than among the lower or working classes.

The pursuit of success implies that high value is placed upon education as a means of mobility. Consistent with this assumption some writers have noted the negative valuation of intellectualism among the lower classes. The emphasis among the stable working class appears to be on utility and pragmatism. As such, the working-class person is interested in end results which are concrete and tangible. Words and intellectual speculation which do not lead to immediate, practical ends are devalued. This disdain for intellectualism appears to stem from modes of reasoning and types of interaction which are threatening and not understood by working-class individuals.[67]

Another value difference among the social classes is reflected in the nature of the social relations which are preferred. The lower-class person is more likely to establish what might be called person-to-person relationships rather than role-to-role relationships. He is oriented to persons as individuals in particularistic terms and does not as a rule relate to persons in terms of the roles they enact. This orientation, which is centered around the person in his total being, stresses subjective and intimate ties in contrast to the more objective, and distant ties found in role-to-role relations. In turn, it understandably leads to a preference for the familiar and predictable, and may partly account for the reluctance of lower-class persons to get out into the world and meet strangers.[68]

This distinction may also help to explain the tendency among the lower-class individuals to stick together. The close, huddled, and intimate conditions of life among the lower classes tend to contribute to the ethic of reciprocity. Thus, their interaction has been described as a kind of mutual insurance scheme where mutual aid and support are available in times of need. As such, the working-class person is more at home in primary group relationships where existing resources are mutually shared. Unlike the middle-class person he is not at home in secondary, segmented and formalized relationships.[69]

A third dimension on which classes have been found to vary is in their valuation of time. Variations occur in the attention given to the past, in the use of the present, and in planning for the future. A reverance for the past is evidenced in a kind of traditionalism which has been largely associated with the working classes. Perhaps, though, a more apparent behavior distinction exists with respect to how time is used in the present, with its implication for the future.[70]

In a national survey of high school students, it was found that lower-class values favored impulse gratification in contrast to the middle-class deferred gratification pattern. The tendency among the middle class person was to save, postpone, and renounce a variety of gratifications with a view towards the future.[71] On the other hand, the working-class person tended to follow what has been called the hedonistic ethic of living it up and following impulses, rather than saving for a rainy day. This general theme has been stressed as a lower-class "way of life" among underprivileged workers.[72]

Perhaps some writers have overstressed the incapability of lower-class persons to defer gratification. Such a view frequently leads to the belief that the lower classes are immoral, uncivilized, promiscuous, lazy, etc. This view has been criticized because it tends to depict lower-class behavior in middle-class value terms and judgments.[73] More study is needed before any final conclusions can be reached in regard to this. But the middle-class emphasis on the constructive use of free time and preparation and planning for the future is known. In essence, the middle-class conception is that time is a commodity which ought not be wasted by random and idle play.

The literature which has been reviewed demonstrates that an intimate relationship does exist between values and class behavior. Doubtless, the concept of social class behavior as it is understood in modern day theory would lose much of its intelligibility were it divorced from the notion of value differences. The evidence that values affect patterns of behavior and thoughts of people in all areas cannot be doubted. But it is not likely that one can neatly classify all individuals,[74] according to value differences.

Although characteristic values may be associated with different classes, very little evidence exists to show that there are "delinquent values."[75] Our view of the deviant system--as a rejected system defined in terms of the mobile and traditional systems--makes it even more difficult to arrive at any consistent set of value distinctions. In fact it is very likely that many of the values which are held by deviant system members are not easily identified because so much of their behavior is instrumentally devised to cope with status deprivation, newcomer status, neighborhood rejection, or whatever. In this sense, the behavior of deviant system members is obscured by their lack of commitment to any consistent value stance. Deviant values vary instrumentally and depending on the situation take on middle or working-class attributes. Until it can be established that values determine behavior or behavior determines value there will in all likelihood continue to be discrepancies regarding this matter.[76]

It may be concluded that middle and working-class values can be measured with suitable instruments. The measurement of deviant values is not an easy matter, however. It may be more helpful to view the expression of deviant values in terms of behavior which incurs negative reactions from others.[77]

Descriptive Typology

For purposes of this study and based on the discussion above, three major value orientations have been identified. These are defined as existing, achieving, and conflicting, each reflecting the neighborhood subsystems which were already discussed.

Existing value orientation:--Individual values held by members of the traditional subsystem are described as existing. The emphasis in general is on being what one is with no overbearing push to compete or achieve. The basic themes of the working-class subculture conform roughly to the existing value orientation as defined here. The person is viewed as being traditional, old-fashioned, somewhat religious and patriarchal. While he prefers a good standard of living he is not attracted to the middle-class style of life with its accompanying concern for status and prestige. In the main there is a reduced striving for success and the emphases is on getting-by rather than getting-ahead, or to exist rather than to achieve. In addition, persons with this value orientation are intense in their relationships, person-centered rather than role-centered, pragmatic and somewhat anti-intellectual in their outlook.

Achieving value orientation:--Achieving values refers to those individuals who adhere to a middle-class ethic which stresses achievement and success. In contrast to individuals who hold existing values which stresses being oneself, the emphasis among the achieving is on doing and aspiring to better oneself.[78] Achieving values refer generally to a set of community accepted preferences, usually associated with middle-class behavior. Individuals are future orientated, value formal education, are role-to-role orientated, take individual responsibility for behavior, and otherwise anticipate occupational and economic advancement.

Conflicting value orientation:--For purposes of this study, negative societal reactions resulting from non-conforming and conflictual behavior constitute a sufficient condition for delineating persons who hold a conflicting value orientation. While many have serious problems of adjustment, not all would necessarily present problems if they lived in other neighborhoods. It is, therefore, the negative societal reaction of the other subsystems, traditional and mobile, that continues to set them apart as non-conformists. Individual values appear to be instrumentally employed and thus resemble existing and achieving orientations in mixed forms. Strictly speaking then, a conflictual orientation refers to deviant behavior styles. Insofar as the satisfactions, preferences, and desires of the deviants can be measured as a system of values they will appear in mingled forms.

In addition to the fact that value differences exist within the subsystems, it can be observed that under particular conditions there is considerable overlapping so that these subsystems appear to be one homogeneous unit. For example, in respect to race relations, the more prejudicial (white backlash) position of the traditional system may be linked with the erratic instrumental behavior of the deviant, and the

14

protective aspirant motivations of the mobile to form a consistent re-action impervious to outside intervention.[79] On the other hand, when members of the mobile subsystem withdraw from extremist racially in-spired hatreds they are sustaining certain boundary maintenance behav-iors which are consistent with their major middle-class aspirations. Likewise, the traditional subsystem members may withdraw into organized resistance against outside intervention when open conflict would be dis-astrous. On the other hand, the deviants, who instrumentally carry out their roles relative to the sanctions or reactions of the other two sub-systems are caught in a dilemma and may very likely act out the dilemma by entering into overt, extremist activity.

Family Types

Theoretical Perspective

The basic American family structure is generally typified as being isolated, and nuclear, consisting of father, mother, and offspring shar-ing the same household as one unit. The strength of the nuclear family appears to be related to its relative independence and adaptability to the requirements of a highly industrialized society. While the family has lost some of its economic, educative, and protective functions, it is not waning in its influence. The family continues to play an import-ant role in relation to the development of its members. Although there is disagreement regarding the exact functions the family fulfills, it is generally agreed that its functions include procreation, status placement, biological and emotional maintenance, and socialization.[80]

Of particular interest to us here is the functioning of the family during the child rearing period in the life cycle. The most obvious significance of the isolated, nuclear type family in this regard is the strong emotional dependency, especially in the parent-child relationship. This is in marked contrast to other family types where there are strong and multiple kinship ties beyond the isolated conjugal unit. Because of the relative absence of extended kinship ties as intervening factors, the life history of the isolated, nuclear type family, its ups and downs, accidents, illnesses, etc., is seen to have a more singular and drama-tic impact on the character formation of the children.[81]

The differentiation of family types by the degree of isolation from related kin is an important distinction. Much of the literature deals with the structural arrangements of nuclear and extended families to de-termine whether these patterns are functional or dysfunctional in rela-tion to other social units. It is becoming increasingly clear that the properties of the nuclear family are not the same for all segments of society. Variations within this ideal type have been found to exist within different socio-economic strata. Considerable differences are also related to regional, racial, and ethnic factors.

When the family is viewed as a social system which confers upon its members a status position in relation to the wider social system, we are viewing it as a critical unit within the social class system. The individual is involved simultaneously in both the family and a so-cial class structure. Their functions differ, however, in that the fa-mily acts as a primary training institution or "factory" for developing personalities,[82] while the social class system is basically a ranking mechanism whereby people are ordered. Generally, it is understood that the point of origin in the status system for an individual is the family into which he is born.

Drawing on various community studies, Hollingshead[83] summarizes class differences in family stability and finds that extended kinship groups exist among the "established" upper classes. The solidarity of the kinship group is reinforced by inherited wealth and intraclass marriage. Such families are viewed to be stable. In contrast, the "new" upper class family with recently acquired wealth is less stable in that it often lacks acceptance at the top of the status system. The practice of conspicuous consumption and "high living" leads to insecurity and family instability and the pressures for upward mobility tends to divide the kinship group. Among the middle classes, there is a relative absence of an extended kinship group. Self discipline, job pressures, and a middle-class morality which includes striving for achievement and success within a framework of family respectability helps keep the nuclear family together. A greater amount of family instability is found among the working class. Such families are in a sense products of the conditions in which they live for they are most often subjected to business fluctuations as wage earners. A job is taken as a necessity rather than as a career. Crises draw extended kin together for mutual assistance and help, although the sharing of meager resources among extended kin leads to tensions and strains. The lower classes exhibit the most family instability of any class in the status structure. Community studies show that these families are most often broken by separation, divorce, death, desertion, and the like. Economic insecurity and "amoral behavior" appear to be most characteristic of this class.

It has been useful to distinguish between lower-class families and stable working-class families. The lower-class family is often identified by its "female-based" household or "matrifocal" form. Such families, found most often among Negroes, consist of one or more related females of child-bearing age and their children. Because of high rates of desertion, illegitimacy, early male mortality, and other factors, much of the direction and authority in the family rests with the mother. The adult male or males, whether father or lover, occupy marginal positions.[84]

The most dominant distinguishing feature of the working-class subculture is the "family circle." The working-class person views life from this circle. The outside world is seen with detachment and distrust. Work is of secondary importance in comparison. Individual achievement and advancement when it runs counter to the solidarity of the family circle is ignored or openly rejected. Regardless of the particular form the family circle takes, that is whether friends are included, or just the classic intergenerational extended kin, Gans states,

> What matters most--and distinguishes this subculture from others--is that there be a family circle which is wider than the nuclear family, and that all of the opportunities, temptations, and pressures of the larger society be evaluated in terms of how they affect the ongoing way of life that has been built around this circle.[85]

Intimately tied to the class differences among family types are ethnic differences which have been found to exist. Studies of Italian-American communities have consistently demonstrated the solidarity or "familism" of Italian families.[86] In the main the Italian family is characterized by a strong sense of unity and feeling for the family group, preference for family values, the confining of personal satisfactions and interests within the family, mutual assistance among family members, and the emphasis on the family's good name, honor, and ideals. One guiding motif is to remain free from strangers and, as such, the family is far more important than the community. In the field of crime, family loyalty and ties have been found to be efficient and functional. The Appalachian Racket Meeting was accordingly described as one "great family picnic."[87]

The class factor is being dealt with as a more significant variable in current studies of family structure. More comparative studies in which class is held constant should help to clarify existing differences in family patterns among ethnic groups.

The middle-class subculture is centered around the nuclear family and its desire to make its way in society. While there are contacts with relatives, individuals derive most of their emotional gratifications and social outlets within the nuclear unit itself. Furthermore, since the outside world is seen to support its aims, no distinction is made between the outside world and the nuclear family as is done by working-class individuals.

Theoretical interest in the sociological study of the family centers primarily on the nuclear family and industrialization. Early studies were impressed with the effects of urbanization on the nuclear family. In this respect, Wirth pointed out how the city substitutes secondary group experiences in the place of primary groups. The effects on the family were to strip it to its barest functional essentials. "The family as a unit of social life is emancipated from the larger kinship system group characteristic of the country."[88] Thus, relationships based on the extended family disintegrate in the city. Parsons theorizes that the nuclear, isolated family is ideally suited to the demands of occupational and geographical mobility which is inherent in modern society. While the bonds exist between the nuclear family and other relatives, these are seen to lack significance for the maintenance of the individual connugal family.[89]

Empirical studies have produced contradictory evidence regarding these hypotheses.[90] Litwak convincingly demonstrates the existence of a "modified extended family."[91] In objection to Parson's view that the nuclear family is the only functional type of family in modern industrialized society, his studies of middle-class wives in Buffalo illustrates that the modified extended family also was consistent with modern industrial society. In contrast to the classical extended family, the modified extended family is not based on authority relations but is more equalitarian in nature. Furthermore, it does not require geographical propinquity or occupational nepotism. The family ties differ from those of the nuclear family in that significant aid is provided in areas of housing, illness, leisure-time pursuits, etc.[92]

Vestiges of the extended family continue to persist, however, and are associated with the working-class subculture and with certain ethnic groups. Such family patterns are most prevelant in older and relatively stable neighborhoods. When members of these families become mobile, the extended family patterns tend to disintegrate.[93]

17

Kinship networks of mutual aid are found to be viable and functional. Sussman discovered that affectionate and economic aid still linked generational families, adding stability to their relationship. Middle-class families evidenced considerable mutual help patterns and were not as isolated or as independent as theorized. The role of the family kin network was supportive of the relationships within the nuclear family. The major activities linking the network were mutual aid and social activities. Mutual aid included exchange of services, gifts, advice and financial assistance. Social activity included family visits, recreational and ceremonial activities. A variety of other services which linked families were mutual services in shopping, escorting children, concern for older persons, scouting jobs for kin, etc. Significantly, related kin sought help from each other rather than from an "outside agency."[94]

In conclusion, empirical studies have not supported clear cut distinctions between the nuclear and extended family patterns in relation to social class factors. Perhaps the viewpoint presented by Cohen and Hodges contrasting lower and middle-class families in this regard more nearly states the case. According to them middle-class couples reinterpret and reorganize kinship ties after marriage in such a way as to promote a mutually gratifying and effective network of relations. The lower classes by contrast tend to maintain kinship solidarities previously formed. As they point out,

> In short, the essential contrast is perhaps not so much
> one of a lower class extended kinship system <u>versus</u> a mid-
> dle-class structurally isolated nuclear family, as it is one
> of tenacity, in the lower class, of <u>individual</u> kinship net-
> works, overlapping but not identical, and relatively resist-
> ant to change <u>versus</u>, in the middle class, reorganization of
> the networks of both spouses in the interest of the solidarity
> and primacy of the conjugal unit.[95]

Furthermore, if these ideal types are considered in terms of separate or combined households, the distinction loses its meaning for virtually all families maintain separate households. Obviously, the truly extended family pattern is also unlikely to exist where there are so few opportunities or occasions in relation to which related kin are required to function together as an economic unit.

Descriptive Typology

For our purposes, however, we will theoretically distinguish between the <u>nuclear</u>, <u>expanded</u>,[96] and <u>mixed</u> family types. The major distinguishing characteristic is reflected in the isolation versus mutual help and association themes. The nuclear type refers to the situation where the family more often centers around its immediate members, providing a more narrow core of affection and maintaining relative isolation and independence from other kin. The expanded type refers to a more intimate grouping of relatives extending beyond the immediate family who share similar interests and mutually assist each other in dealing with day-to-day problems of living. The kind of problems dealt with by the expanded type include mutual financial help, care of children, decision-making at times of illness and death, and a variety of other mutual services which members are obligated to perform for each other. By definition, the expanded family type would most likely be associated with the traditional subsystem. The mixed family type is defined relative to the other two. It is perhaps best characterized by its inconsistent behavior and cannot be viewed as either nuclear or expanded.

We can now consider family types as they differ according to the previously described major subsystems and value orientations. Our view of the family as a social system is substantially the same as for the various group types which were discussed.[97] That is, the family as is true of the peer group should be viewed in terms of its functions. As Homans pointed out so well, kinship relations are not maintained unless they serve some purpose for those involved.[98]

We are not concentrating here, however, on the functions the family provides for its members but rather on how the family form or structure functions by virtue of the fact that it is a part of one subsystem as against another. Broadly speaking, the family differences which have been found in the literature comparing social classes should be expected to exist in comparing subsystems within a single social class, since in the final analysis these subsystems are viewed as prototypes of the class structure of the wider society.

Expanded Family:--The family constellation in the working class traditional subsystem would be expected to reflect patterns which may in a sense be considered to be functionally suited to meet the needs which subsystem members have in common. For example, since financial resources are limited, the family patterns are somewhat extended to insure mutual financial support and protection. In the traditional working-class family, then, we would expect to find extended family networks or systems which are effectively organized for mutual support and backing. When the neighborhood code calls for one or another relative to fulfill certain functions, rarely does he neglect to do so. The mutual obligations and responsibilities would account in large measure for the organization, intimacy and control which is so characteristic of stable working-class neighborhoods.

Nuclear Family:--Members of the mobile subsystem have different needs. They share certain features which are typical of the middle class. It is not surprising, therefore, to expect that the type of family most often found in this subgroup would be of the nuclear variety. In a sense, the greater abundance of internal resources (e.g. money, better jobs, etc.) makes them less dependent upon each other as compared to the traditional subsystem. While there are some extended family ties, these would not be as intense, and mutually binding. Their values which stress independent achievement would also indicate a family type which does not hamper the social or geographical mobility of its members. On the other hand, the isolated conjugal family in this subsystem acts as a stronger control on the young and does not rely on the help of "other families" or on neighborhood controls.

Mixed Family:--It is anticipated that the family type which characterizes the deviant subsystem would demonstrate considerable inconsistency. There would not be a significant or effective system of mutual obligations, expectations or support in these families as compared to those in the traditional subsystem. This would be so because by definition members of the deviant subsystem are not able, for one reason or another, to measure up to such stringent requirements. Generally, the family status position is lower and may more often be characterized by instability and lack of access to economic and social resources. It may

19

also be found that the deviant family will show certain features similar to those of the mobile system families, such as isolation. Unlike the mobile system families, however, such families are not likely to be able to move socially into the outer society.

In conclusion, then, it may be simply stated that the interaction of individual values, group properties, and family types are intertwined.[99] An analysis of the major subsystems cuts across these variables and reveals some characteristically patterned interactions or social system attributes. On this basis it would be expected that similarity in value orientation would be related to similar peer group types and similar family forms in the same subsystems. Moreover, a comparison or functional analysis of the three interacting subsystems would explain why certain characteristic features will be maintained. A knowledge of the linkages among these factors would permit the analytic observer to predict behavior expectations in a more systematic and comprehensive manner. Perhaps the most unique point of departure in this theoretical perspective is that no longer is it permissible for certain levels of analysis to accept the conception that the so-called "old ethnic" neighborhood is one homogeneous system. Insofar as the social configuration is explicated and made visible in specific terms, our ability to understand the meaning of behavior will be greatly enhanced.

Statement of Hypotheses

We have stated that the purpose of this study is to determine to what extent boys with similar value orientations will belong to similar families and be members of similar type peer groups. In light of the formulation presented above, we can state the following hypotheses:

Hypotheses Regarding Value Orientations and Family Types

I. Boys with existing values will belong to expanded type families.

II. Boys with achieving values will belong to nuclear type families.

III. Boys with conflicting values will belong to mixed type families.

Hypotheses Regarding Value Orientations and Group Types

I. Boys with existing values will be members of corner-boy groups.

II. Boys with achieving values will be members of college-boy groups.

III. Boys with conflicting values will be members of deviant-boy groups.

Hypotheses Regarding Value Orientations, Family Types, and Group Types

I. Boys with existing values will belong to expanded type families and be members of corner-boy groups representative of the traditional subsystem.

20

II. Boys with achieving values will belong to nuclear type families
     and be members of college-boy groups representative of the mobile
     subsystem.

III. Boys with conflicting values will belong to mixed type families
     and be members of deviant-boy groups representative of the deviant
     subsystem.

     The independent variable, namely value orientation, will be shown
to have a relationship to the dependent variables of family type and
group type. The hypotheses state that there will be an association between these variables. It does not suggest a cause and effect relationship. Furthermore, the hypotheses are limited to detecting the
qualities or characteristics of the variables as they are patterned a-
mong the boys. While the subsystems are assumed to be dynamic and
functionally operative there is no effort to test this here. This remains for subsequent research after it is established that the attributes under study in fact exist as hypothesized.

FOOTNOTES--CHAPTER I

[1]The Italian-American community is typically viewed in the litera-
ture as a homogeneous social structure. See, for example, Irvin Child,
Italian or American? The Second Generation in Conflict (New Haven:
Yale University Press, 1943), William F. Whyte, Street Corner Society:
The Social Structure of an Italian Slum (2d ed. rev.; Chicago: University of Chicago Press, 1955) and Herbert Gans, The Urban Villagers:
Group and Class in the Life of Italian Americans (Glencoe, Illinois:
The Free Press of Glencoe, 1962). All three sources distinguish various adaptations: Child identifies three types of ethnic "reactions"
among Italian-American males: in-group, rebellion and apathetic; Whyte
differentiated "corner boys" and "college boys" both of which are products of working-class families and neighborhoods but with vastly different values; Gans identifies four class related behavior styles among
Italian-American adults which are termed mobiles, maladjusted, routine
seekers, and action seekers. While such distinctions were made these
studies tend to treat the neighborhood as if it were a homogeneous unit
by stressing those typically unique qualities such as close-knit organization, strong neighborhood controls, family and peer group domi-
nation, etc. all of which have come to typify the Italian-American Community in the literature.

[2]Modern texts in social stratification include: Joseph A. Kahl,
The American Class Structure (New York: Rinehart and Company, Inc.,
1957); Leonard Reissman, Class in American Society (Glencoe, Illinois:
The Free Press, 1959); and Harold Hodges, Social Stratification: Class
in America (Cambridge, Massachusetts: Schenkman Publishing Company,
Inc., 1964). For a useful book of readings see Reinhard Bendix and
Seymour Martin Lipset (eds.), Class, Status, and Power: A Reader in
Social Stratification (Glencoe, Ill.: Free Press of Glencoe, 1953).

[3]Karl Marx and Friedrich Engels, Manifesto of the Communist Party
(New York: International Publishers, 1922).

[4]H. H. Gerth and C. Wright Mills (trans. and ed.), From Max Weber:
Essays in Sociology (New York: Oxford University Press, 1946). While
Weber's overshadowing influence is recognized, very little has been
done to test his concepts empirically. See Reissman, op. cit., p. 69.
Others have expanded or refined the three dimensions: Kaare Svalastoga, "Social Differentiation" in Robert E. L. Faris (ed.), Handbook of
Modern Society (Chicago: Rand McNally and Co., 1964) p. 536 adds education as a fourth major criteria. In light of empirical studies, Kahl,
op. cit., pp. 8-12, refines Weber's scheme to include six variables--
namely, personal prestige, occupation, possessions, interaction, class
consciousness, and value orientations.

[5]Robert S. Lynd and Helen Merrell Lynd, Middletown (New York:
Harcourt, Brace and Company, 1929) and Middletown in Transition (New
York: Harcourt, Brace and Company, 1937) analyzes social classes large-
ly in terms of occupational and economic differences. W. Lloyd Warner
and Paul S. Lunt, The Social Life of a Modern Community (New Haven:
Yale University Press, 1941), and Yankee City Series, volumes I through

22

IV plus a variety of others in the "Warner School: emphasize status differences. Participation and acceptance are viewed as strong associated factors. John Dollard, Caste and Class in a Southern Town (New Haven: Yale University Press, 1937) focuses on psychological correlates of the social structure. James West, Plainville, U.S.A. (New York: Columbia University Press, 1945) sees class divisions based on "rank" or status which are closely related to particular behavior patterns. August Hollingshead, Elmtown's Youth (New York: John Wiley and Sons, Inc., 1949) demonstrate how adolescent behavior parallels the class structure of the adult world.

[6]The functional theory of social stratification is presented largely in two papers: Talcott Parsons, "A Revised Analytical Approach to the Theory of Social Stratification" in Bendix and Lipset, op. cit., pp. 92-128; and Kingsley Davis and Wilbert E. Moore, "Some Principles of Stratification: A Critical Analysis," American Sociological Review, X (April, 1945) pp. 242-49. The major opposing views and criticisms can be found in Melvin Tumin, "Some Principles of Stratification: A Critical Analysis," American Sociological Review, XVIII (August, 1953), 387-94; Richard Simpson, "A Modification of the Functional Theory of Stratification," Social Forces, XXXV (December, 1956) 132-38; Walter Buckley, "Social Stratification and the Functional Theory of Social Differentiation," American Sociological Review, XXIII (August, 1958) 369-75; and Dennis W. Wrong, "The Functional Theory of Stratification: Some Neglected Considerations," American Sociological Review, XXIV (December, 1959) 772-82.

[7]For a most penetrating synthesis of functional sociology see Robert K. Merton, Social Theory and Social Structure (Rev. and enl. ed. Glencoe, Illinois: The Free Press, 1957).

[8]Charles Loomis, Social Systems: Essays on Their Persistence and Change (Princeton, New Jersey: Van Nostrand Co., 1960).

[9]Ibid., p. 5.

[10]Ibid., p. 32.

[11]A classic description of such controls can be found in Whyte, op. cit.

[12]Leaders in the traditional subsystem may be termed "locals" while those in the mobile may be termed "cosmopolitan." See Merton, op. cit., pp. 393-420.

[13]"Social reaction" occupies a central place in Lemert's theory of social deviation. See Edwin Lemert, Social Pathology: A Systematic Approach to the Theory of Sociopathic Behavior (New York: McGraw-Hill Book Co., Inc., 1951), Chap. 3.

[14]The concept of subculture is used here to refer to a subdivision of the main culture comprised of a combination of class status, ethnic background, urban residence, and regional residence which form a functioning unit with an integrated impact on participating individuals. See Milton M. Gordon, Social Class in American Sociology (Durham, North Carolina: Duke University Press, 1958), p. 254. The use of the term subsystem would be applicable when the reference is to "patterned interactions." Charles Loomis, op. cit., p. 3.

[15]In this sense, this analysis is like a sociogram where an individual's affective ties by definition will reveal something about other individuals who share such ties.

[16]Richard Cloward and Lloyd Ohlin, Delinquency and Opportunity: A Theory of Delinquent Gangs (Glencoe, Illinois: The Free Press, 1960), p. 7.

[17]Welfare Federation of Cleveland, "Patterns of Groupings Within the United Youth Program", A report prepared for the Subcommittee to Study the Needs of Emotionally Disturbed Delinquent Adolescents (Cleveland: Welfare Federation of Cleveland, 1959).

[18]Edwin H. Sutherland and Donald R. Cressey, Principles of Criminology (6th ed.; New York: J. B. Lippincott Company, 1960), p. 613 uses the term near delinquent in referring to the child who is on the verge of becoming a delinquent. Practitioners have used the term pre-delinquent usually to describe children with symptoms such as enuresis, temper tantrums, sullenness, timidity, and the like. This is misleading in that it connotes a sense of finality. The use of the prefix "pre" is more appropriately used in a definite developmental sense as seen for example in the term pre-adolescent.

[19]Albert Cohen, Delinquent Boys: The Culture of the Gang (Glencoe, Illinois: The Free Press, 1955).

[20]Whyte, op. cit., p. xx.

[21]Cohen, op. cit., pp. 128-30.

[22]Ibid., p. 129.

[23]Cloward and Ohlin, op. cit. Partial support of this theory can be found in Irving Spergel, Racketville, Slumtown, Haulburg: An Exploratory Study of Delinquent Subcultures (Chicago: University of Chicago Press, 1964) pp. 122-23. It was found that access to means are in fact differentially distributed according to the kind of neighborhood in which delinquency was found. There was an intimate connection between socially organized system of opportunities and delinquent subcultures. In "Racketville" the prevalent activity was criminal, in "Slumtown" it was conflict, and in "Haulburg" it was theft.

[24]Walter B. Miller, "Lower Class Culture as a Generating Milieu of Gang Delinquency," Journal of Social Issues, XIV, No. 3 (1958) 5-19.

[25]See David J. Bordua "Delinquent Subcultures: Sociological Interpretations of Gang Delinquency" The Annals of the American Academy of Political and Social Science, CCCXXXVIII (November, 1961), 119-36.

[26]The natural history of the gang was described some time ago by Frederic M. Thrasher, The Gang: A Study of 1,313 Gangs in Chicago (Chicago: The University of Chicago Press, 1927), pp. 69-76. In his view, age differentials revealed the "gang child," "gang boy," and "gang man."

[27]Similarly one can project to corresponding adult peer groups (e.g. middle class "clubs," working class "lodges," or deviant "syndicates") which serve as adult models or reference groups. One does not

of course need to be a member of the group for it to serve as a reference group. Such identifications and linkages may cross subsystem boundaries. For example, older corner-boys who are "tough" and "know their way around" may have a special significance for the potential delinquent boys who are younger and are still groping for a solution to adjustment problems.

[28] A word of explanation is required here to avoid an overly mechanistic viewpoint. While it may be that similar adjustment problems (status/deprivation) are of importance with some members, others may of course be drawn into the group for a variety of reasons. Also, as in most groups, some members may be marginal, becoming central around certain issues, activities, or affairs. Other individuals may command central positions in the group, enjoying high status positions which do not necessarily carry delinquent roles. It happens, therefore, that when delinquent acts are committed, they are by no means completely sanctioned by all the members.

[29] A. Paul Hare, "Interpersonal Relations in the Small Group," in Faris, op. cit., pp. 239-40.

[30] Merton, op. cit., p. 309. Theodore M. Newcomb, Ralph H. Turner, and Philip E. Converse, Social Psychology: The Study of Human Interaction (New York: Holt, Rinehart and Winston, Inc., 1965), pp. 357-58, state that to qualify as a group property; an attribute must apply to the group as a single entity, it must be variable, and it must be susceptible to measurement.

[31] Merton, op. cit., pp. 310-26.

[32] The small group is usually taken to number from two to twenty. Thrasher, op. cit., analyzes gangs that number as large as 2,000. He found, however, that the two-boy gang or pal relationship acted as a primary structure shaping the growth of the gang. For an edited version of the size of gangs see Fredric M. Thrasher, "The Gang" in A. Paul Hare, Edgar F. Borgatta, and Robert F. Bales, Small Groups: Studies in Social Interaction (New York: Alfred A. Knopf, 1961) pp. 38-44. One must also distinguish between absolute and relative size. Merton, op. cit., pp. 312-13, points out that groups with the same absolute size will function differently depending upon their size relative to other groups in the same "institutional sphere."

[33] Georg Simmel, "The Number of Members as Determining the Sociological Form of the Group" American Journal of Sociology, VIII, (July, 1902) 1-46, and 158-96.

[34] P. E. Slater, "Contrasting Correlates of Group Size" Sociometry, XXI (June, 1958) pp. 129-39. In this connection, Michael Argyle, The Scientific Study of Social Behaviour (London: Methuen and Co., Ltd., 1957), p. 123 concludes that there must be a common need which is satisfied to a greater degree by membership in smaller groups.

[35] Paul H. Fischer, "An Analysis of the Primary Group," Sociometry, XVI (August, 1953) 272-76.

[36] Newcomb, Turner, and Converse, op. cit., p. 363.

[37] Hare, loc. cit., pp. 254-55.

[38]Kurt H. Wolff (trans. and ed.), The Sociology of Georg Simmel (Glencoe, Illinois: The Free Press, 1950), pp. 87-93. The term "permeability" is also used to indicate degree of ready access to membership. Operationally, it is reflected by the absence of entrance requirements and the degree to which membership is solicited. See, for example, John K. Hemphill, Group Dimensions: A Manual for Their Measurement (Columbus, Ohio: The Ohio State University, 1956) pp. 15-40.

[39]Merton, op. cit., p. 265 and p. 293.

[40]Harold D. Lasswell and Abraham Kaplan, Power and Society: A Framework for Political Inquiry (New Haven: Yale University Press, 1950) p. 35. See also Ernest van den Haag, Passion and Social Constraint (New York: Stein and Day, 1963) p. 100, who states that intensive ties among members is often associated with exclusiveness among groups; but, when groups accept newcomers readily, the bonds "which are so easily lengthened often become less stringent."

[41]Dorwin Cartwright and Alvin Zander (eds.), Group Dynamics: Research and Theory (2nd ed.; Evanston, Illinois: Row, Peterson and Co., 1960), p. 73, hypothesize that group attractiveness is related to the degree that it is likely to meet the desires and needs of its members. For other discussions of factors affecting membership in groups see Edwin J. Thomas, "Theory and Research on the Small Group: Selected Themes and Problems" in Leonard S. Kogan (ed.), Social Science Theory and Social Work Research (New York: National Association of Social Workers, 1959), pp. 93-96; and Newcomb, Turner and Converse, op. cit., pp. 309-21.

[42]Murray Hausknecht, The Joiners: A Sociological Description of Voluntary Association Membership in the United States (New York: The Bedminster Press, 1962), pp. 21-22.

[43]Leon Festinger, Stanley Schachter, and Kent Back, Social Pressures in Informal Groups: A Study of Human Factors in Housing (Rev. ed.; Stanford, California: Stanford University Press, 1963). See also Theodore Newcomb, The Acquaintance Process (New York: Holt, Rinehart and Winston, 1961).

[44]Hemphill, op. cit., p. 2-4, for example, uses at least four dimensions: control, intimacy, participation and potency, all of which seem to get at the concept of engagement in varying degrees. On the other hand, "Involvement Activity" is considered to be a basic variable common to interacting persons by Edgar F. Borgatta and Leonard S. Cottrell, Jr., "On the Classification of Groups," Sociometry, XVIII (December, 1955), 409-22.

[45]Merton, op. cit., p. 311.

[46]See Gans, op. cit., p. 37; Whyte, op. cit., p. 255-76; and Richard Hoggart, The Uses of Literacy: Changing Patterns in English Mass Culture (Boston: Beacon Press, 1961), pp. 68-73.

[47]See Lewis Yablonsky, "The Delinquent Gang as a Near Group" Social Problems VII (Fall, 1959) pp. 108-117, and Lewis Yablonsky, The Violent Gang (Baltimore, Maryland: Penguin Books, 1966) especially Chapter 13 and 14. See also Harold W. Pfautz, "Near Group Theory and Collective Behavior: A Critical Reformulation," Social Problems IX

(Fall, 1961) pp. 167-174.

[48]Terence K. Hopkins, The Exercise of Influence in Small Groups (Totowa, New Jersey: The Bedminster Press, 1964) p. 184, revealed centrality to be related positively to rank, observability and conformity each of which had a "persisting impact on the distribution of influence among the members of small groups." In contrast, John W. Thibaut and Harold H. Kelly, The Social Psychology of Groups (New York: John Wiley and Sons, Inc., pp. 70-72, point up the functional utility of easy peripheral accessibility to groups. Potentially unstable relationships can be developed with relative impunity as a transition to more stable relationships at a relatively "low cost." For a rather thorough analysis of social regulations that determine the "individual's conceptions and allocations of involvement" see Erving Goffman, Behavior in Public Places: Notes on the Social Organization of Gatherings (Glencoe, Illinois: The Free Press, 1963), Chap. 4.

[49]Festinger, Schachter, and Back, op. cit., pp.164-66, define cohesion as the total field of forces acting on members to remain in a group; Cartwright and Zander, op. cit., p. 72, see it as group "attraction"; while Argyle, op. cit., pp. 123-24, defines it in terms of the extent to which members like each other.

[50]Neal Gross and William E. Martin, "On Group Cohesiveness," American Journal of Sociology, LVII (May, 1952) 546-54. See also Warren O. Hagstrom and Hanan C. Selvin, "Two Dimensions of Cohesiveness in Small Groups," Sociometry, XXVIII (March, 1965) 30-43. For example, groups may be attractive without having intimate personal ties binding members together.

[51]Kurt W. Back, "Communications in Experimentally Created Hierarchies," Leon Festinger, Jurt Back, Stanley Schachter, H. H. Kelly, and John W. Thibaut, Theory and Experiment in Social Communication (Ann Arbor: Institute for Social Research, University of Michigan, 1950).

[52]Newcomb, Turner, and Converse, op. cit., p. 386.

[53]For a review of significant findings, see Argyle, op. cit., pp. 123-28 and Robert T. Golembiewski, The Small Group: An Analysis of Research Concepts and Operations (Chicago: University of Chicago Press, 1962), pp. 169-70.

[54]These terms should not be confused with value orientations and behavior styles of group members as described by White, op. cit., p. 97 and Cohen, op. cit., p. 104. While it is expected that these relationships will be demonstrated, the terms are used to describe group forms and have been selected for clarification in terms of the overall study.

[55]These characteristics may of course be dysfunctional for its individual members as well. The corner-boy does not break away easily from his group. A good example of this was related by a corner-boy to the writer. He was complaining that he lost out on a job opportunity when his friends (corner-boy group) accompanied him to the interview. In his own words, "They acted like bums casing the joint, so the boss never even gave me a chance."

[56]Whyte, op. cit., pp. 273-74. Similarly, Hoggart, op. cit., pp. 238-49, describes the "Scholarship boy" as one who is more and more

alone as he breaks with his working-class origins.

[57]This distinction is developed in Albert S. Alissi, "Social Influences on Group Values", Social Work, X (January, 1965), 14-22. A distinction must also be made between values and norms. While the interlapping of the two is not clear, norms usually refer to standards or rules that state what human beings should or should not think, say, or do under certain circumstances. See Judith Blake and Kingsley Davis, "Norms, Values, Sanctions" in Faris, op. cit., p. 456-64.

[58]Herbert H. Hyman, "The Values Systems of Different Classes: A Social Psychological Contribution to the Analysis of Stratification" in Bendix and Lipset, op. cit., p. 438.

[59]Genevieve Knupfer, "Portrait of the Underdog," in Bendix and Lipset, op. cit., p. 263.

[60]William H. Sewell, Archie O. Haller, and Murray Straus, "Social Status and Educational and Occupational Aspiration," American Sociological Review, XXII (February, 1957), 67-73.

[61]Albert K. Cohen and Howard M. Hodges, Jr., "Characteristics of the Lower-Blue-Collar-Class," Social Problems, X (Spring, 1963), 322.

[62]S. M. Miller and Frank Riessman, "The Working Class Sub-Culture: A New View, "Social Problems, IX (Summer, 1961), 91-92. See also Kahl, op. cit., pp. 205-10.

[63]Bernard C. Rosen, "The Achievement Syndrome: A Psychocultural Dimension of Social Stratification," American Sociological Review, XXI (April, 1956), 203-211.

[64]Bernard C. Rosen, "Race, Ethnicity, and the Achievement Syndrome" American Sociological Review, XXIV (February, 1959), p. 53. However, social class and ethnicity were found to interact in influencing motivation, values, and aspirations.

[65]Merton, op. cit., Chap. 4.

[66]Rosalind Gould, "Some Sociological Determinants of Goal Strivings," Journal of Social Psychology, XIII (May, 1941), 470-71. Other factors appear to be operative as well. See, for example, LaMar T. Empey, "Social Class and Occupational Aspirations: A Comparison of Absolute and Relative Measurement," American Sociological Review, XXI (December, 1956) 703-709 where it is reported that relative aspirations of lower class high school seniors preferred and anticipated higher occupational statuses than their fathers. Richard P. Boyde, "The Effect of the High School on Students' Aspirations," American Journal of Sociology, LXXI No. 6 (May, 1966) pp. 628-39, examines high school composition as an intervening variable affecting students' aspirations. Whyte, op. cit., described two sets of standards for advancement--in local neighborhoods, and in wider society. A person cannot advance in both in the Italian community which he studied.

[67]Miller and Riessman, loc. cit., p. 94; Cohen and Hodges, loc. cit., p. 318; Hodges, op. cit., 209-10. See also Seymour Martin Lipset, Political Man, The Social Bases of Politics (Garden City, New York: Doubleday and Company, Inc., 1960), pp. 115-20.

[68]See Miller and Riessman, loc. cit., pp. 93-94 and Cohen and Hodges, loc. cit., p. 316. Gans, op. cit., pp. 89-103 distinguishes between object-centered and person-centered orientations among the "West Enders" in an Italian-American Community. Role orientations are foreign to West Enders which in part explains their distrust of the outside world. Erving Goffman, The Presentation of Self in Everyday Life (Garden City, New York: Doubleday and Company, Inc., 1959) p. 128 uses the dramaturgical analogy to describe person-to-person orientations in terms of "backstage language" where the person can be himself and engage others in an easy and relaxed manner.

[69]Many writers have made the contrast where individual responsibility of the middle classes stand in opposition to the reciprocity among the lower classes. See Cohen, op. cit., p. 96-97; Cohen and Hodges, op. cit., p. 307; and Hoggart, op. cit., p. 69.

[70]Hoggart, op. cit., pp. 157-61.

[71]Louis Schneider and Sverre Lysgaard, "The Deferred Gratification Pattern: A Preliminary Study," American Sociological Review XVIII (April, 1953), p. 143. On the other hand, Murray A. Straus, in "Deferred Gratification, Social Class, and the Achievement Syndrome," American Sociological Review, XXVII (June, 1962) 326-35, found little evidence to support the hypothesis that socio-economic status and deferred gratification were associated.

[72]See Hodges, op. cit., pp. 205-206; Hoggart, op. cit., p. 110; and Allison Davis, "The Motivation of the Underprivileged Worker" in William F. Whyte (ed.), Industry and Society (New York: McGraw-Hill Book Co., 1946), p. 103.

[73]Hyman Rodman, "On Understanding Lower Class Behaviour." Social and Economic Studies, VIII (December, 1959), p. 444. In another paper he suggests that the lower classes have a wider range of values and a lower degree of commitment to them. See Hyman Rodman, "The Lower Class Value Stretch," Social Forces, XLII (December, 1963), 205-15.

[74]Cohen, op. cit., p. 105-109, cites, for example, a study by Barker where working-class and middle-class boys were asked to respond to value questions involving dilemma which could be resolved by either the corner-boy or college-boy preferences. Although there were some differences, many inconsistent responses were given.

[75]No satisfactory list of delinquent values exists. Witness, for example, one prepared by Frederick Meyers, Our Troubled Youth: Education Against Delinquency (Washington, D. C.: Public Affairs Press, 1959), p. 26. Milton L. Barron, "Juvenile Delinquency and American Values" American Sociological Review, XVI (April, 1951), p. 212, concludes that studies of value differentials between delinquents and nondelinquents are "insignificant and contradictory."

[76]A most recent study of gangs, non-delinquent corner boys, and middle class boys in Chicago, attempted in part to measure value differences. Generally, in all groups measured the middle class style of life was highly valued. Hypotheses regarding gang values were generally not substantiated. See James F. Short and Fred L. Strodtbeck, Group Process and Gang Delinquency (Chicago: The University of Chicago Press, 1965) Chap. 3.

[77]Lemert, _supra_, offers a purely "sociological" interpretation of how such reaction evolves.

[78]This distinction is fully elaborated in Florence Kluckhohn, and Fred. L. Strodtbeck, _Variations in Value Orientations_ (Evanston, Illinois: Row, Peterson and Co., 1961) pp. 15-17.

[79]Some of these particular characteristics can of course be explained in terms of minority behavior, having some clearly distinguishable Italian ethnic overtones. For example, living in "Little Italy" tends to magnify the in-group as against the out-group. This localization as well as Americanization conjoin to produce a kind of climate that persistently rejects other minority status groups. See Richard Schermerhorn, _These Our People_ (Boston: D. C. Heath and Co., 1949), Chap. II.

[80]Talcott Parsons and Robert F. Bales, _Family, Socialization and Interaction Process_ (Glencoe, Illinois: The Free Press, 1955) pp. 16-22; and Talcott Parsons, "The Kinship System of the Contemporary United States" in Herman D. Stein and Richard A. Cloward, _Social Perspectives on Behavior_ (Glencoe, Illinois: The Free Press, 1958), pp. 7-19.
Useful references which treat the family in social terms includes Norman W. Bell and Ezra F. Vogel (eds.), _A Modern Introduction to The Family_ (Glencoe, Illinois: The Free Press of Glencoe, 1960); and Rose Laub Coser, ed. _The Family: Its Structure and Functions_ (New York: St. Martin's Press, 1964).

[81]Margaret Mead, "The Contemporary American Family as an Anthropologist Sees It," in Stein and Cloward, _op. cit._, pp. 25-26.

[82]Parsons and Bales, _op. cit._, p. 16.

[83]August B. Hollingshead, "Class Differences in Family Stability," in Stein and Cloward, _op. cit._, pp. 45-52.

[84]Raymond T. Smith, _The Negro Family in British Guiana: Family Structure and Social Status in the Villages_ (London: Routledge and Kegan Paul, 1956) pp. 221-28, points out that this marginality is related to class and the degree to which the father contributes to the status and support of the family. See also, E. Franklin Frazier, "The Negro Family in the United States" in Stein and Cloward, _op. cit._, pp. 53-57 and Walter B. Miller, "Implications of Lower Class Cultures for Social Work" _The Social Service Review_ XXXIII No. 3 (September, 1959), 219-36.

[85]Gans, _op. cit._, p. 245.

[86]Paul J. Campisi, "The Italian Family in the United States" in Stein and Cloward, _op. cit._, pp. 77-79, presents a table suggesting a continuum from the unacculturated old world familism to an American type. He notes that some of the older patterns persist. Other comparative studies show family influences to differ in ethnic cultures. For example, Jewish values favoring education, individual achievement, and mobility were found to be markedly different from the Italian familism and fatalism. See, Fred L. Strodtbeck, "Family Interaction, Values, and Achievement," in D. C. McClelland, A. Baldwin, U. Bronfenbrenner, and F. Strodtbeck, _Talent and Society_ (Princeton: D. Van Nostrand, 1958) pp. 135-194. Nathan Glazer, _American Judaism_ (Chicago: University

of Chicago Press, 1957) points out how in contrast to the Italians, the Jews did not try to limit their children from participating in the outside world.

[87] Nathan Glazer and Daniel Patrick Moynihan, Beyond the Melting Pot: The Negroes, Puerto Ricans, Jews, Italians, and Irish of New York City (Cambridge, Massachusetts: The M.I.T. Press and Harvard University Press, 1963) p. 196. See also Edward Banfield, The Moral Basis of a Backward Society (Glencoe, Illinois: The Free Press, 1958).

[88] Louis Wirth, "Urbanism as a Way of Life" American Journal of Sociology, XLIV (July, 1938), p. 21.

[89] Talcott Parsons, "Revised Analytical Approach to the Theory of Social Stratification," in Bendix and Lipset, op. cit., pp. 92-128, and Talcott Parsons, "The Social Structure of the Family," in Ruth N. Ashen (ed.), The Family: Its Functions and Destiny, (New York: Harper and Bros., 1949), pp. 191-92.

[90] See Morris Zeldith Jr. "Family, Marriage and Kinship" in Faris, op. cit., pp. 723-28.

[91] Eugene Litwak, "Occupational Mobility and Extended Family Cohesion," American Sociological Review, XXV (February, 1960), pp. 9-21, and Eugene Litwak, "Geographic Mobility and Extended Family Cohesion," American Sociological Review, XXV (June, 1960), pp. 385-94.

[92] Four Family types are identified as extended, modified extended, isolated nuclear, and dissolving. The modified extended ". . . might be the most effective in the maintenance of a democratic industrial society." Eugene Litwak, "Extended Kin Relations in An Industrial Democratic Society" in Ethel Shanas and Gordon F. Streib, Social Structure and the Family: Generational Relations (New Jersey: Prentice-Hall, Inc., 1965), p. 323. Irving Rosow, "Integenerational Relationships: Problems and Proposals," Ibid., suggests that the modified extended family may be in effect an intermediate stage which is leading to a nuclear type in the future. Zeldich, loc. cit., p. 726, uses the term "expressive kindred" to apply to networks of families who do not act as a whole in any occupational sense but continue mutual help patterns.

[93] For descriptions of mutual assistance patterns among English working-classes, see J. M. Mogey, Family and Neighborhood (Oxford: The Clarendon Press, 1956 and Michael Young and Peter Willmott, Family and Kinship in East London (London: Routledge and Kegan Paul, 1957) cited in Zelditch, loc. cit., p. 726. See also, Lee Rainwater, Richard P. Coleman, and Gerald Handel, Workingman's Wife: Her Personality, World and Life Style (New York: Oceana Publications, Inc., 1959) who stress the greater importance of relatives among working-class women in contrast to middle-class women. According to Frances J. Woods, The American Family System (New York: Harper and Brothers Publishers, 1959) mutual aid within the family is a lower-class characteristic deriving largely from economic necessity.

[94] Marvin Sussman, "The Help Pattern in the Middle Class Family." American Sociological Review XVIII (February, 1953), 22-28. See also, Harry Sharp and Morris Axelrod, "Mutual Aid Among Relatives in an Urban Population" in Ronald Freedman, et al., Principles of Sociology, (rev. ed.; New York: Henry Holt and Company, 1956), 433-39. Marvin

Sussman and Lee Buchinal, "Kin Family Network: Unheralded Structure in Current Conceptualizations of Family Functioning" Marriage and Family Living XXIV (August, 1962), p. 235. For a table showing major forms of help and direction of service between parent and offspring see Marvin Sussman, "The Isolated Nuclear Family: Fact or Fiction," Social Problems VI (Spring, 1959), 338-40.

[95]Cohen and Hodges, loc. cit., p. 309.

[96]Pitkin used the term expanded differently to describe families who have taken in a relative. See Donald Pitkin, "Land Tenure and Farm Organization in an Italian Village (Harvard University: Unpublished Ph.D. Dissertation, 1954), p. 114, as cited and discussed by Gans, op. cit., p. 46.

[97]While both families and groups are viewed as social systems, there are, of course, many differences. In contrast to the peer group the family is age heterogeneous, has a longer "tradition," closer affective ties, etc. In terms of functions S. N. Eisenstadt, From Generation to Generation: Age Groups and Social Structure (Illinois: The Free Press, 1956), pp. 40-46, advances the thesis that the "age-homogeneous" peer group arises where the family "age-heterogeneous" group cannot insure the attainment of full social status of its members. The age-homogeneous groups function to facilitate the person's entrance into the society-based social system. Parsons and Bales, op. cit., pp. 299-306, in tracing the process of differentiation note that instrumental and expressive functions within the family are similar to the specialization found in small groups.

[98]George C. Homans, The Human Group (New York: Harcourt Brace and Co., 1950), pp. 268-80.

[99]Parsons and Bales, op. cit., p. 33, develop the thesis ". . . that neither personalities nor social systems can be adequately understood without reference to culture, to each other and to the relations of these three to each other." It does appear that in a similar way, groups and families as social systems and individual values as cultural phenomena are constantly interacting and are inextricably intertwined. Thus knowledge of one can make for predictions in the others, or changing one will bring about changes in the others.

CHAPTER II

METHODS AND PROCEDURES

Overview of the Study Design

The research was conducted in a small Italian-American neighborhood known as "Little Italy" consisting of about 4,200 people, and which is perhaps best characterized by its physical and social isolation from the wider Cleveland community. This neighborhood earned a reputation during the prohibition days as a tough and close-knit area where sharp distinctions between insiders and outsiders existed. More recently, its negativism towards outside intervention resulted in physical violence and rioting in connection with the civil rights struggle.

The writer became intimately acquainted with the community and its problems in his capacity as resident director of a settlement house located in the neighborhood. Eight years with the settlement has provided him with many opportunities to know and work with almost every boy who lived in the neighborhood. Under the auspices of the settlement, which enjoys a long-standing trust and confidence with the neighborhood residents, the data were gathered in a relaxed and natural way. It is unlikely, in fact, that the desired cooperation would have been achieved by any "outside" agency.

The study involved every boy age twelve through eighteen who was living in the neighborhood at the time. Names were drawn largely from the files of the two local elementary schools and a junior high school. Since every neighborhood boy, with a few exceptions would have at one time or another attended these schools, enrollment cards were used to identify the majority of the sample. Graduation records of the past four years supplied the additional names of older boys, fifteen through eighteen who might attend schools outside the neighborhood but were still residents.

Older boys who may have graduated from schools outside the neighborhood, but more recently moved into the neighborhood were traced through settlement house files and through information supplied by other boys. Actually, very few boys were in this category since fewer families with teen-agers move into the neighborhood. Instead, the tendency is for families to move out of the neighborhood.[1]

By cross referencing the data, 239 boys were identified who lived in the neighborhood at the time of the study. Each boy was given a paper-pencil type value test. Questionnaires were administered to groups of boys meeting at the settlement house. In each instance, the researcher read each item aloud along with the boys to minimize reading and comprehension difficulties. This test, titled the "What Do You Think Questionnaire" contained value statements designed to discriminate between existing and achieving orientations among the boys.

Independent of this procedure, a second procedure was adopted whereby judges reviewed every boy known to them to distinguish between conforming and non-conforming boys. On the basis of written criteria describing value preferences and behavior styles each conforming boy was rated by the judge as to whether he held an existing or achieving value orientation. The non-conforming or conflicting category represented negative reactions as determined by independent ratings of the judges.

By combining the two procedures, a study group of 95 boys of which roughly one-third were classified as being in each of the three value categories, was finally determined. Fairly intensive interviews were then held with the parents of these boys to gather information on family patterns. The mothers of the boys served as the major source of information. It was possible to interview only about half of the fathers. Thus, their interviews served only as a crude check on the data received from the mothers.

A final paper-pencil test was completed by each boy individually. This was administered by the investigator and was called the "Describe Your Group Questionnaire". It was designed to reveal near sociometric data, group associations, and individual preferences regarding peer group membership. In every case, each item was read aloud to facilitate understanding. Care was also taken to assure the boys of anonymity.

Other supporting data on peer group membership and associations were obtained from agency files, key neighborhood informants, and field notes describing the investigator's observations of boys in groups. Since almost every boy was known to the investigator, it was possible to make cross references which in effect served as checks on the data. In the main, the sponsorship[2] of the agency proved to be extremely helpful as respondants were found to be receptive and cooperative.

In summary, the research design was as follows: a sample of boys was screened by an objective values test and judges' ratings to determine basic value orientations of existing, achieving, and conflicting. Parents of these boys were interviewed to gather data on the family. The boys themselves gave an accounting of their groups, friendship ties, and the like. Supplementary information from regular agency records was utilized at various times to support these data. Treating individual values as the independent variable, and family and group characteristics as the dependent variables, comparisons were made to determine patterned differences.

Measurements

Value-orientations

No standardized value scale was found which could be used to discriminate boys according to achieving and existing orientations. It is surprising that there are no measures of middle-class values which for our purposes would approximate the achieving orientation. As one writer concludes, ". . .sociologists have not produced an instrument which seems as basic to much of their research as the intelligence test is to psychological research."[3] Similarly, Miller and Riessman have observed how difficult it is to conceptualize the stable working-class culture.

They state, for example, that they were ". . .unable to develop a parsimonious conceptualization, such as a non-deferred gratification pattern which attempts to explain by this single formulation or theme a
vast array of behavior."[4] Other instruments such as the Srole's anomie
"A" scale or the California "F" scale of authoritarianism also appeared
to be inadequate for the same reason.[5]

Other objective indicators typically employed in social stratification studies were considered but quickly abandoned because they were
too indirect and imprecise. Occupation of the father, house type,
source of income and other measures have been used to advantage in other studies; but, values do not necessarily vary with these characteristics. The use of such indicators to approximate life styles or value
orientations may be misleading. In fact, discrepancies in comparative
studies of social class behavior may be traced to inaccurate categorization instruments. For example, contradictory evidence concerning mutual help patterns in American families may be explained in terms of
the use of indicators which fail to differentiate social class accurate-
ly. In any event, the need here is for a direct measure of the boys'
values; and, an instrument needed to be specifically designed to do
this.

The "What Do You Think Questionnaire" was finally developed from
a variety of sources: Kluckhohn and Strodtbeck[6] offer a classification
of value orientations which in part served as an outline for comparing
values. They start by assuming that there are a limited number of common human problems which all people must solve at one time or another.
Solutions are seen to vary within a range of possible alternatives.
These alternatives are differentially preferred in varying societies,
some being more dominant than others forming a rank order of choices.

Five human problem areas are singled out in the form of questions
to which the answers vary in different societies. These questions and
the range of solutions are given as follows:

1) What is the character of innate human nature? (evil or good)

2) What is the relation of man to nature? (subjected to nature,
    in harmony with nature, or master over nature)

3) What is the temporal focus of human life? (past, present, or
    future)

4) What is the modality of human activity? (being, being-in-
    becoming, or doing)

5) What is the modality of man's relationship to other men?
    (lineality, collaterality, or individuality)

Viewed in these terms, Kluckhohn and Strodtbeck find that the American middle-class orientation stresses the belief that human nature is
evil but mutable, that man has mastery over nature, there is a future
orientation, a doing philosophy, and an individualistic relationship to
others.[7]

On the basis of monograms, literary material and personal observations, Kluckhohn categorized Italians in the Boston area.[8] The values
that the newly arrived Italians held were that human nature was both

good and evil, man was subjected to nature, he was present-time orientated, held a being philosophy, and was collateral in his relationship to others. In most cases, middle-class values were less acceptable and third in order of preference.

The search for appropriate items to be incorporated in the value questionnaire was extended to other writers.[9] Rosen's achievement syndrome[10] provided some help. He explains differential rates of mobility of racial and ethnic groups in terms of dissimilar psychological and cultural orientations towards achievement. The achievement syndrome is measured by three component parts: achievement motivation, achievement values, and educational-occupational aspirations. Achievement motivation as measured by the TAT was seen to be beyond the scope of this study. Educational-occupational aspirations were incorporated into the parents' interviews. The achievement values which were culturally induced corresponded with Kluckhohn's material and were a useful guide upon which to build.

The majority of the items were adapted most directly from Cohen,[11] Clark and Winninger,[12] and Miller and Riessman.[13] Comparisons of middle class and stable working-class boys are made by Cohen where differing standards are in evidence. In part, the middle-class boys are seen to use free time constructively, have long range plans, believe in personal advancement and individual responsibility. The stable working-class boy does not use his free time constructively, has short-run interests, believes in primary group solidarity, and interdependency. Clark and Wenninger developed an instrument of goal orientation incorporating basic societal values, lower-class focal concerns, and middle-class standards. Included were thirty items related to such things as success, achievement, individuality, staying out of trouble, seeking excitement, being smart, planning ahead, working hard, etc. Miller and Riessman's descriptions of stable working-class themes were also useful in developing the questionnaire. They stress the person-centeredness, pragmatism, stability, traditionalism, excitement and intensity of the stable working-class person.

From these sources an initial list of over one hundred value statements was devised. This list was finally reduced to eighteen items after a long period of informal discussions with a variety of boys. Ambiguous concepts were dropped, duplications of items were eliminated, and changes in vocabulary were made so that the statements would be simple, clear, and relevant to the boys in their actual living circumstances.

This eighteen-item questionnaire was pretested with twenty-one junior and senior high school boys from another neighborhood. Judged by their leaders to be typical achieving boys with middle-class orientations, these boys were selected from a YMCA program. The neighborhood had a large Italian population and was similar in many respects to Little Italy. At the same time the questionnaire was similarly tested with a few boys from the study area who were judged by the investigator to be typical neighborhood working-class boys. These boys were not expected to be in the study group since they did not meet the age requirements.

The pre-test procedure used was as follows: The investigator briefly explained his interest in learning what boys believed. After reading the instructions, as they appeared on the forms, he read each

statement in order. Each boy separately circled the response he selected. After administering the entire questionnaire the boys were
asked to comment on any questions which were unclear or confusing.
Wherever the investigator doubted that the question was understood, he
explored its meaning by asking the boys to rephrase it in their own
words. During this process items that failed to discriminate adequately or were confusing were dropped from the questionnaire.

A questionnaire of fourteen statements was finally selected to be
used as the major categorization instrument.[14] These were made up of
seven pairs of items representing contrasting value orientations stated
in such a way that each boy was afforded the opportunity to respond
positively or negatively to the same value expression. These contrasting value orientations along with their corresponding value statements
were as follows:

Existing Values

1. Present-Time Orientation...... "It's best to live for today
and not worry about tomorrow."

2. Person-to-person Centered..... "If I were an usher at a movie,
I would let my friends in free."

3. Group Solidarity.............. "No matter what happened, I
would always stick with my own
clique."

4. Short-run Interests.......... "I don't stay interested in the
things I do but I soon get
bored and look for something
else to do."

5. Being Philosophy............. "If I had nothing to do I would
just hang around."

6. Spontaneous use of time....... "I don't waste time planning
what to do because I can always
find something at the last minute."

7. Pragmatism................... "Reading books and studying is
mostly a waste of time because
you really learn from experience."

Achieving Values

1. Future-Time Orientation....... "People should give up things
and sacrifice to be ready for
the future."

2. Role-to-role Centered........ "If I were elected president of
an organization, I would treat
everyone according to the rules
--even my friends."

3. Individual Responsibility..... "Every guy should be responsible for himself and not expect
   the guys in the clique to cover for each other."

4. Long-term Plans.............. "I'm already doing things now
   for what I want way in the fu-
   ture."

5. Doing Philosophy............ "The most important thing in
   life is to be able to do things
   well."

6. Planned use of Time.......... "I like to sit down, talk and
   plan things to do with my free
   time."

7. Intellectualism.............. "People with a lot of education
   give the best advice about
   life."

The boys were allowed four possible responses to each statement--
strongly agree (YES), agree (yes), disagree (no), and strongly disagree
(NO). Each answer was assigned a point value with the higher points
given to achieving responses. Scores ranged from zero (most existing)
to seventy (most achieving). This questionnaire therefore served to assess value orientations and preferences and was used to differentiate
the most existing and most achieving boys.

Another measure was employed to insure the accuracy of the final
categorization of the boys. Independent judges were asked to review
each boy they knew in the study and rate him according to criteria descriptive of the value preferences and behavior styles characterizing
the value orientation categories. The concurrence of a majority of
judges' ratings was required before any designation was made. The
judges' ratings were then used to distinguish between existing, conflicting, and achieving boys. Written instructions were provided to serve
as a standardized guide in rendering judgements.[15]

The results of both the "What Do You Think Questionnaire" and the
judges' ratings were combined to yield the final study groups. Where
a boy held a high achieving score on the values test and was judged by
judges to be achieving, he was so designated and included in the study
group. Similarly, where a boy held a low score on the values test and
was judged by judges to be existing, he was so designated and included
in the study group. In no case was either an achieving or existing boy
included in the final study group unless he had been similarly categorized by both of these measures.

The major distinguishing factor used to designate the conflicting
boys was their non-conforming behavior relative to the other two designations. The scores achieved on the "What Do You Think Questionnaire"
were not used in any way to distinguish conflicting boys. But rather
these designations were determined solely by judges' agreements and reflected negative societal reactions regarding the boys' behavior.

Based on the results of the "What Do You Think Questionnaire" and
the verification by independent judges' ratings, thirty-seven achieving

and twenty-six existing boys were designated. In addition, judges' ratings delineated thirty-two conflicting boys.

Parent's Interviews

Another major instrument[16] was the parent's interview schedule administered to parents and designed to get information about the boys' families. It was composed of a number of parts and included basic identifying background data, the nature of relationships to kin, mutual help patterns, and neighborhood and community contacts which were both formal and informal.

It was particularly important to have information about the family's background for comparative purposes to insure that all the boys did in fact come from similar working-class origins. Basic identifying data included age and sex characteristics, marital status, ethnic and religious affiliations, and educational and occupational achievement of the respondants. Family background included birthplace of parents and grandparents, education and occupation of male kin, length of residence in the neighborhood, etc. Other questions were asked to gain some understanding of the social class position of the family. These included data on the dwelling unit, family income,[17] educational and occupational aspirations for children, and estimates of social class position.

To determine the type and degree of intimacy which existed among relatives related to each family, a four-way classification system was employed. The system was previously used by Bott[18] in her intensive field study of families in England. Any given relationship between two relatives is termed intimate, effective, non-effective, or unfamiliar based on the intimacy of the contact and the degree of knowledge one has of the other. Intimate refers to a relationship which is very close with a great deal of contact and knowledge. Effective refers to a relationship which is not as close, but where contact is maintained and one has a knowledge of another's general interests, tastes, and the like. The unfamiliar relationship describes the type where there are practically no contacts, but basic identifying facts were known. The unfamiliar refers to a relationship where nothing is known beyond the fact that the relative exists. Generally this framework was incorporated into a chart form[19] in the schedule listing the number of all relatives both in the family of orientation and procreation. This chart also indicated the place of residence of all kind.

Other questions were asked to determine how the family functioned. Respondants listed occasions when family gatherings were held and how inclusive such events were. Visiting patterns with relatives were also ascertained. A number of questions were asked to determine the areas where mutual help among family, relatives and friends existed. These related to decision-making and sources of help in times of trouble, mutual aid with finances, with care of children, and with personal problems.

Finally, questions were asked about neighborhood and community contacts. Some referred to informal friendship patterns and ties with neighborhood people. Others referred to formal membership in organizations and clubs. A few questions were developed specifically to get an indication of the degree of identification with the neighborhood.

Twelve different interviewers were hired to administer the parents' interviews. This group consisted of trained social workers, social work students, agency staff members, an agency board member, a librarian and a school teacher. Each person was in no way previously connected with the study, and had to be familiarized with the basic goals and objectives of the research. An initial schedule was pretested by about one half of the judges with parents from the neighborhood who were not in the study group. Some questions were reformulated, some were dropped as a result of this process. Through group conferences the judges were in most instances easily trained to conduct the interviews. They were assigned cases randomly having no knowledge as to the designated value orientation of the boy. Except in only two instances, a separate interviewer was used whenever both the father and mother of the same family were interviewed.

Cases were selected in such a way that similar proportions of parents were interviewed from all the available cases in the three groups. In all, one-hundred and five persons were interviewed -- each home visit lasting from one-half to an hour and a half in length. Thirty-eight parents of existing boys were interviewed; twenty-seven conflicting; and forty achieving.

Group Properties Questionnaire

A final major measurement was used to compare the boys in their natural peer groups and was known as the "Describe Your Group Questionnaire". To observe all of the groups directly was considered to be beyond the resources of the study. It was possible, however, to use the boys themselves as informants to get data on how they viewed their own groups. Agency records of organized group activities, containing membership and attendance features, were therefore also available.

The "Describe Your Group Questionnaire" contained questions focused on factors such as group size, membership characteristics, degree of cohesion or solidarity, and degree of engagement of members in the group.

It was pretested with a number of neighborhood boys not included in the final study group before it was prepared in its final form. The procedure used was similar to that employed in developing the value-orientation questionnaire. In this case, however, boys were administered the questionnaire individually. Each item was read by the investigator after which the boys were asked to raise questions concerning ambiguous items. In some cases they rephrased the statement or question so as to be more relevant and understandable.

The final form of the questionnaire[20] was then administered to seventy-nine[21] boys--those who were in the study group and still living in the neighborhood. Each interview lasted from ten to twenty minutes. This was a rather smooth procedure since the investigator read each statement along with the respondent and was able to give directions as the need arose. Care was taken to guarantee anonymity and enlist cooperation. The investigator knew most all the boys which was of considerable help.

The actual questionnaire consisted of five parts which were somewhat overlapping in content: The first section was concerned with group membership. Boys were asked to list the members of their group or "crowd". In addition, they were asked to indicate marginal members, new members, and personal friends who were not members. The second section presented a variety of statements to determine the degree and kind of cohesion which was attributed to the group. These referred to the personal attraction of members, similarity of personal goals, pride in membership, amount of sharing and stick-to-getherness, personal satisfaction in being in the group and so forth. Other statements in this section dealt with how easy it was to become a member, how visible the group was, and its meaning to the respondent. The third section dealt with the kinds of activities the group engaged in either as a whole or in part. Of special interest was the amount of time the boys spent in such activities as an indicator of the degree of engagement required of group members. The fourth section presented profiles of life-like situations which were in essence dilemmas pitting the group against other forms of allegiance such as family, friendships, money, success, and status. These alternative choices were designed also to give additional data on cohesion and engagement in the group. The fifth and final section required expressions of personal preferences from the boys concerning their concept of the ideal group or club. Responses elicited information concerning group size, open or closed nature of groups, purposes and goals, length of the life of the group, degree of freedom as individuals or as members of cliques, amount of loyalty to be expected, etc.

In summary, the following number of interviews were conducted: The "What Do You Think Questionnaire" which served as the primary categorization instrument was administered to all 239 boys who lived in the neighborhood. Similarly, judges' ratings were made on all of the 239 boys who were known. After the boys were differentiated according to value orientations, their parents were interviewed. A total of sixty-eight Mothers (twenty-four Traditionals, eighteen Deviants, and twenty-six Mobiles) and thirty-seven Fathers (fourteen Traditionals, nine Deviants, and fourteen Mobiles) were interviewed in all. The "Describe Your Group Questionnaire" was administered independently to each boy by value orientation. A total of seventy-nine boys were so tested (twenty-five Existing, twenty-seven Conflicting, and twenty-seven Achieving).

Characteristics of the Sample

The concept of the homogeneous neighborhood is based on the premise that people with similar backgrounds will develop similar modes of interaction which will typify the neighborhood as a whole. The hypotheses to be tested question this assumption and assert that in reality diverse patterns of interaction will develop in spite of similar class backgrounds. More specifically, not all boys with similar working-class backgrounds will reflect stable working-class orientations.

To insure that the sample was not biased with respect to the boys' backgrounds, boys were compared according to ethnic and religious affiliations, origin of parents, education and occupation of male kin, and length of residence in the neighborhood.

Generally, nationality and religious backgrounds for all groups in the sample were found to be similar. The largest difference was between the traditional and mobile fathers in respect to their Italian heritage. However, in view of the small numbers involved and the lack of any significant statistical difference, one could conclude that the boys came from the same ethnic and religious groups.

TABLE 1[a]

PROPORTION OF PARENTS WHO ARE ITALIAN BY
SUBSYSTEMS

	Mothers			Fathers		
	Traditional (24)	Deviant (18)	Mobile (26)	Traditional (14)	Deviant (9)	Mobile (14)
Percent Italian	.75	.53	.77	1.00	.77	.64
Percent Other	.25	.47	.23	.00	.23	.36

[a]Unless otherwise indicated, tables presented throughout this study are essentially comparisons of respondants differentiated by value orientations of the boys in the study group. For all comparisons, the use of the subsystem terms, Traditional, Deviant, and Mobile, will be used.

TABLE 2

PROPORTION OF PARENTS WHO ARE CATHOLIC BY
SUBSYSTEMS

	Mothers			Fathers		
	Traditional (24)	Deviant (18)	Mobile (26)	Traditional (14)	Deviant (9)	Mobile (14)
Percent Catholic	.92	.78	.81	.86	.77	.79
Percent Other	.08	.22	.19	.14	.23	.21

No significant differences were found concerning birthplace of parents. Only a small difference was observed between the traditional and the mobile. Roughly the same proportion of mothers and fathers were born in the neighborhood as in Italy. This is also true of the grandparents except that an usually high proportion of the traditional paternal grandparents were from Italy (.86). Frequencies among the deviants show only a smaller proportion (.11) of mothers and no fathers who were born in the neighborhood.

Table 3 on the following page provides the statistics on birthplaces of parents and grandparents by subsystems.

When parents of the boys were compared to determine how many had lived their childhood in the neighborhood, no significant differences were found. These data are contained in Table 4.

Generally, educational levels do not indicate any large differences among parents and grandparents. A comparison of subsystems reveals some percentage differences but these are not statistically significant. Table 5 indicates the amount of education of parents and grandparents by subsystems.

With respect to occupational background, small differences did appear between these groups. These were greater among grandparents than among fathers. Surprisingly, a larger proportion (.50) of traditional grandfathers occurs in the Craftsmen and Foremen category, while the mobiles have a greater proportion (.65) in the Services and Laborers category. However, in view of the small number involved and the lack of any statistical differences, it can be concluded that occupations of male kin taken as an indicator of social class reveal the groups to be from the same general background. Table 6 contains the data showing occupations of fathers and grandfathers.

A final comparison was made to determine how long families had maintained residence in the neighborhood. While the percentage of traditional families with longer residence in the neighborhood is slightly higher, the differences were not found to be significant. On the average, over three-fourths of the entire sample lived in the neighborhood over ten years. This in itself demonstrates a generally stable population which is characteristic of the neighborhood as a whole. The shorter time that deviants and mobiles were in residence in the neighborhood was also seen although the percentages were found to be too small to indicate statistical significance. Table 7 shows the length of time parents lived in the neighborhood.

In conclusion, it has been shown in the foregoing mentioned tables that the sample was in fact drawn from the same "working-class" population. When boys were compared according to the general social class variables as outlined, no significant differences were found.

TABLE 3

BIRTHPLACES OF PARENTS AND GRANDPARENTS BY
SUBSYSTEM

Place of Birth	Mothers			Fathers		
	Traditional (24) %	Deviant (18) %	Mobile (26) %	Traditional (14) %	Deviant (9) %	Mobile (14) %
Neighborhood	.33	.11	.35	.50	.00	.36
Cleveland	.13	.33	.04	.07	.22	.07
U.S. (not Cleveland)	.33	.39	.27	.36	.33	.29
Italy	.21	.11	.19	.07	.22	.14
Other Country	.00	.06	.11	.00	.22	.00
Unknown	.00	.00	.04	.00	.00	.14
	Maternal Grandfathers			Paternal Grandfathers		
Neighborhood	.13	.00	.00	.07	.00	.07
Cleveland	.00	.05	.00	.00	.00	.07
U.S. (not Cleveland)	.13	.39	.19	.07	.22	.29
Italy	.62	.39	.65	.86	.67	.57
Other Country	.04	.05	.08	.00	.11	.00
Unknown	.08	.11	.08	.00	.00	.00
	Maternal Grandmothers			Paternal Grandmothers		
Neighborhood	.04	.00	.08	.07	.00	.00
Cleveland	.04	.06	.08	.00	.00	.14
U.S. (not Cleveland)	.17	.44	.15	.00	.22	.36
Italy	.67	.50	.61	.86	.67	.43
Other Country	.04	.00	.08	.00	.11	.00
Unknown	.04	.00	.00	.07	.00	.07

TABLE 4

PROPORTION OF PARENTS WHO LIVED THEIR CHILDHOOD IN
THE NEIGHBORHOOD BY SUBSYSTEM

	Mothers			Fathers		
	Traditional (24)	Deviant (18)	Mobile (26)	Traditional (14)	Deviant (9)	Mobile (14)
Percent Who Lived Childhood in Neighborhood	.42	.33	.58	.57	.22	.36
Percent Who Lived Childhood Elsewhere	.58	.67	.42	.43	.78	.64

TABLE 5

EDUCATIONAL ACHIEVEMENT OF PARENTS AND GRANDPARENTS
BY SUBSYSTEM

Educational Level	Mothers			Fathers		
	Traditional (24) %	Deviant (18) %	Mobile (26) %	Traditional (14) %	Deviant (9) %	Mobile (14) %
Under 8th Grade	.26	.22	.24	.36	.56	.36
Ninth to Twelfth Grade	.37	.39	.46	.43	.33	.36
High School Graduate	.29	.33	.30	.14	.11	.21
College Incomplete	.08	.06	.00	.07	.00	.00
College Complete	.00	.00	.00	.00	.00	.07
	Maternal Grandfathers			Paternal Grandfathers		
Under Sixth Grade	.33	.39	.54	.43	.56	.50
Seventh to Eleventh	.13	.11	.12	.14	.11	.14
High School Grad.	.13	.11	.15	.00	.00	.00
College	.04	.06	.04	.00	.00	.07
Unknown	.37	.33	.15	.43	.33	.29

45

TABLE 6

OCCUPATIONS OF FATHERS AND GRANDFATHERS BY SUBSYSTEM

Occupation	Fathers			Paternal Grandfathers			Maternal Grandfathers		
	Traditional (19) %	Deviant (16) %	Mobile (22) %	Traditional (14) %	Deviant (9) %	Mobile (14) %	Traditional (24) %	Deviant (18) %	Mobile (26) %
Professional, Proprietors, Clerical	.05	.05	.18	.00	.11	.00	.00	.22	.15
Craftsmen and Foreman	.32	.31	.41	.50	.00	.14	.29	.17	.27
Farmers	.00	.00	.00	.07	.33	.14	.08	.00	.23
Services and Laborers	.63	.63	.41	.29	.56	.65	.54	.50	.31
Unknown	.00	.00	.00	.14	.00	.07	.08	.11	.04

TABLE 7

LENGTH OF TIME PARENTS LIVED IN THE NEIGHBORHOOD BY
SUBSYSTEM

Length of Residence	Fathers and Mothers Combined		
	Traditional (38) %	Deviant (27) %	Mobile (40) %
Under five years	.08	.15	.20
Five to ten years	.08	.15	.07
Ten to twenty years	.24	.26	.23
Over twenty years	.60	.44	.50

FOOTNOTES--CHAPTER II

[1] This is due largely to tensions and anxieties relative to race relations. Teen-agers in particular are affected in that the only public high school which is available to residents is attended predominately by Negroes.

[2] See Appendix A.

[3] Robert H. Bohlke, "Social Mobility, Stratification Inconsistency and Middle Class Delinquency" Social Problems, VIII, (Spring, 1961), 359.

[4] S. M. Miller and Frank Riessman, "The Working Class Subculture: A New View." Social Problems, IX (Summer, 1963), 95.

[5] See Leo Srole, "Social Integration and Certain Corollaries: An Exploratory Study," American Sociological Review XXI (December, 1956), 709-16. For a critique of these scales see Gerhard E. Lenski, and John C. Leggett, "Caste, Class, and Deference in the Research Interview," American Journal of Sociology LXV, (March, 1960), 463-67.

[6] Florence Kluckhohn and Fred L. Strodtbeck, Variations in Value Orientations (Evanston, Illinois: Row, Peterson and Co., 1961). Chap. 1.

[7] Ibid., p. 12.

[8]Florence Kluckhohn "Some Reflections on the Nature of Cultural Integration and Change." Sociological Theory, Values, and Sociocultural Change, (London: Collier-Macmillan Limited, The Free Press, 1963), p. 241.

[9]Kluckhohn and Strodtbeck, op. cit., pp. 80-90 contains twenty-two items where choices are made by respondants in five American Southwest Communities. Only a few of these could be modified or adapted for use with boys.

[10]Bernard C. Rosen, "Race, Ethnicity, and the Achievement Syndrome" American Sociological Review XXIV (February, 1959) 47-60.

[11]Cohen, op. cit., pp. 84-94.

[12]John P. Clark and Eugene P. Wenninger "Goal Orientations and Illegal Behavior Among Juveniles," Social Forces, XXXXII (October, 1963). 54-55.

[13]Miller and Riessman, loc. cit., pp. 90-94.

[14]See Appendix B.

[15]See Appendix C. Six judges recruited mainly from the settlement house staff were used to make these designations. Through group conferences and practice in estimating from sample profiles, the judges were trained to develop a similar frame of reference for making the required designations. This was facilitated by the fact that the format had been used previously and discussed often during staff development sessions; not as a tool of research, but to facilitate an understanding of neighborhood boys and encourage the development of more suitable programs.

[16]See Appendix D.

[17]To deal with this, special 3 x 5 cards were provided the interviewer to hand the respondant. It spelled out by code number incomes by year, month, week or hour. The respondant had only to give the appropriate identifying number.

[18]Elizabeth Bott, Family and Social Network (London: Tavistock Publications Limited, 1964), p. 119-121.

[19]Three by five cards spelled out the four categories of relationships. These were shared with the respondant to facilitate understanding and standardize responses.

[20]See Appendix E.

[21]Only four boys were unavailable at the time of the testing and were therefore lost to the study.

CHAPTER III

FINDINGS

Value Orientations

It became necessary first to designate boys according to the three major value orientations--existing, conflicting, and achieving. The design specified that the sample should consist of the thirty most extreme boys in each category or as near to that number as possible. There were, therefore, no absolute breaking points established for selecting the final sample.

The primary source of information concerning value orientations was derived from the "What Do You Think Questionnaire." Seven pairs of opposing values were presented in fourteen statements to determine value preferences. Since it was recognized that values would not be found to exist in pure form, each statement provided for four possible responses reflecting four levels of agreement and disagreement. These statements were scored from zero to five points each (0, 2, 3, and 5). Total possible scores ranged from zero to seventy points reflecting a continuum of existing to achieving value orientations. Thus, the lowest and highest scores were taken to represent existing and achieving orientations respectively.

The application of this questionnaire along with judges' ratings discriminated 26 boys with existing orientations, and 39 boys with achieving orientations. The criteria of "negative societal reactions" as measured by judges yielded 32 boys with conflicting orientations. Existing boys scored within the range of 22 to 48 with a mean score of 40.00. In contrast, the achieving boys scored within the range of 49 to 59 with a mean of 52.95. Although the conflicting boys were not selected on the basis of their scores; it was found that, as expected, their scores varied the greatest, ranging from 18 to 59 with a mean of 41.45. It was apparent that there was a tendency on the part of all boys to prefer achieving values in that most scores were above the midpoint of 35 on the value continuum.

An internal analysis of the boys' responses to specific value statements made more detailed comparisons possible. Table 8 shows the proportion within each category who answered "YES" or "yes" to each of the value items.

It can be seen that the existing boys had the highest mean of proportions in responding to existing values while the achieving boys had the lowest. Conversely, the achieving boys had the highest mean of porportions responding to achieving values while the existing boys had the lowest.

With respect to the achieving boys, the proportions favoring achieving values and disfavoring their counterparts were consistent in

49

TABLE 8

PROPORTION OF EXISTING, CONFLICTING, AND ACHIEVING BOYS
GIVING A POSITIVE RESPONSE TO VALUE ITEMS IN THE
"WHAT DO YOU THINK QUESTIONNAIRE"

Value Items	Existing (24) %	Conflicting (27) %	Achieving (27) %
Existing Values			
Present-Time-Orientation	.60	.41	.45
Person-to-person Centered	.40	.41	.12
Group Solidarity	.68	.74	.48
Short-run Interests	.52	.63	.29
Being Philosophy	.60	.56	.15
Spontaneous use of Free Time	.40	.26	.15
Pragmatism	.44	.37	.12
Means	.52	.48	.25
Achieving Values			
Future-Time-Orientation	.64	.77	.92
Role-to-role Centered	.76	.92	.92
Individual Responsibility	.56	.52	.81
Long-term Plans	.52	.67	.78
Doing Philosophy	.96	.82	.88
Planned use of Free Time	.60	.86	.81
Intellectualism	.84	.67	.71
Means	.70	.75	.83

every single pair. It appears, therefore, that all of the value statements served in some measure to discriminate achieving boys.

On the other hand, preferences among the existing boys were not as
consistent. Although three value items--group solidarity, a being philosophy, and present-time orientation--were given high preferences ranking among the upper half of those preferred; the existing boys also
tended to favor achieving values. However, relative to the achieving
boys, in every case except two (a doing philosophy and intellectualism)
the percentage difference between the two groups was in the hypothesized
direction.

Further analysis of the sample revealed certain other characteristics which should be noted. The mean age of all boys was 15.7 years.
Conflicting boys were found to be slightly older with a mean age of 16.4,

while the existing and achieving boys had mean ages of 15.4 and 14.9 respectively. Although this represented slight age differences, the age factor was repeatedly analyzed to insure that it did not bias the findings. Except in a few instances which were noted, it was not found to be influential.

TABLE 9

PERCENTAGE DISTRIBUTION OF BOYS ACCORDING TO THEIR AGES BY SUBSYSTEM

Age Categories	Traditional (25) %	Deviant (27) %	Mobile (27) %
Under fifteen	.44	.33	.44
Sixteen and over	.56	.67	.56

$$x^2 = 2.67 \text{ n.s.}$$

Changing residential patterns of the boys were also noted and were found to be revealing. During the testing period, which lasted about a year, the original sample of 97 boys was reduced by 14 boys as a result of their having moved from the neighborhood. Most of these boys had been found to hold achieving and conflicting value orientations. Only one boy held an existing value orientation. Table 10 shows the percentage differences. As expected, this finding suggests that the traditional families are more likely to identify with the neighborhood preferring to remain; and are less mobile or outward orientated.

A comparison of the three groups of boys also revealed some striking differences in their school and work adjustments. Among the existing boys, 88 per cent were attending school, 8 per cent had completed high school and were working, and 4 per cent had dropped out of school. Among the conflicting boys, 53 per cent were still in school and about 47 per cent had dropped out of school. Of these, a few were reenrolled in training programs of one kind or another while most were unemployed or working sporadically. Among the achieving, all were attending school with 11 per cent enrolled in college. Table 11 graphically illustrates how the circumstances of the boys tend to conform to expectations.

Family Types

Before presenting the findings concerning family types, the use of terms should be clarified. The terms existing, achieving, and conflicting, refer to value orientations of the boys and are used to describe individuals. Families are described as expanded, nuclear, or mixed. Peer groups are designated as corner-boy, college-boy, and deviant-boy

TABLE 10

PERCENTAGE DISTRIBUTION OF BOYS IN THE STUDY GROUP
WHO REMAINED OR MOVED FROM THE NEIGHBORHOOD
DURING THE ONE YEAR STUDY PERIOD BY
SUBSYSTEM

Residence	Traditional (26) %	Deviant (32) %	Mobile (39) %
Remained in the neighborhood	.96	.81	.82
Moved from the neighborhood	.04	.19	.18

$$x^2 = 3.21 \text{ n.s.}$$

TABLE 11

PERCENTAGE DISTRIBUTION OF BOYS ACCORDING TO THEIR
SCHOOL OR WORK ADJUSTMENTS BY SUBSYSTEM

School or Work Status	Traditional (26) %	Deviant (32) %	Mobile (38) %
Attending regular schools	.88	.53	.89
Attending colleges	.00	.00	.11
Completed high school and working	.08	.00	.00
Dropped out of school	.04	.47	.00

$$x^2 = 30.83 \quad < .005 \quad 2 \text{ d.f.*}$$

*Test for significance was computed to compare the number of boys in school with the number who dropped out of school.

types. To maintain consistency, subsystem classifications will be used in most cases to organize the data. Consequently, the use of the broader terms to describe the subsystems, traditional, deviant, and mobile, represent combinations of the typologies specified above and are employed to determine the extent to which empirical descriptions hold true. This is done in full recognition of the fact that, strictly speaking, the basis for the original differentiation was the value orientations of the boys.

In summary then, the three subsystems and their designated subparts are as follows: (1) the traditional subsystem--with existing value orientations, expanded family types, and corner-boy peer groups; (2) the deviant subsystem--with conflicting value orientations, mixed family types, and deviant-boy peer groups; and (3) the mobile subsystem--with achieving value orientations, nuclear family types, and college-boy peer groups.

A variety of measures was made to compare family types. We will review these findings in terms of social class factors, kinship ties, family functioning, and community and neighborhood contacts.

Social Class Factors

An examination of the boys' backgrounds, presented earlier, revealed a generally similar working-class background. Although this was so, current living conditions of the families were compared to determine the extent to which they have adopted differential social class attributes.

An examination of family income disclosed that mobile families as anticipated had higher family incomes. The median income among mobile families was $7,000 compared to $5,445 among the traditional and $3,643 among the deviant. Table 12 shows the percentage distribution of families by income.

TABLE 12

PERCENTAGE DISTRIBUTION OF FAMILY INCOMES BY
SUBSYSTEM

Income of the Family	Traditional (22) %	Deviant (17) %	Mobile (26) %
Under $3,000	.09	.41	.00
$3,000 to $5,999	.50	.41	.34
$6,000 and over	.41	.18	.66

$$x^2 = 19.16 \quad < .005$$

Households were also compared to determine the degree of home ownership and type of dwelling unit. Roughly, one-third of all the families owned their own homes. Although the rate of home ownership was slightly higher among mobile families, no significant differences were found. In terms of dwelling units most of the families lived in double houses or small apartment buildings. Very few occupied single houses although the greater percentage of singles were found among the mobiles and deviants. Again, no significant differences were discovered.

Although residential characteristics did not differ greatly, there were other differences found concerning more intangible attributes. For example, educational and occupational aspirations regarding children varied greatly. Mobile families, as reported by mothers, had significantly higher aspirations regarding the education of their sons. Table 13 gives the percentage distribution of mothers' responses regarding their aspirations for their sons' future education. It can be seen that 90 per cent of the mobile mothers desired that their sons complete college in contrast to only 38 per cent of the deviants. On the other hand, the lesser expectations of the traditionals and deviants relative to the mobiles are quite evident. A comparison of mothers' educational aspirations for their daughters revealed similar differences.

TABLE 13

PERCENTAGE DISTRIBUTION OF MOTHERS' EDUCATIONAL
ASPIRATIONS FOR THEIR SONS BY SUBSYSTEM

Educational Desires	Traditional (36) %	Deviant (26) %	Mobile (40) %
To complete high school	.42	.62	.10
To complete college	.58	.38	.90
	$x^2 = 19.90$ $< .005$		

Mothers were also asked to indicate their occupational desires for their sons. Their responses are presented in Table 14. Occupations were roughly divided into two broad categories: professional, proprietary, and managerial; and clerical, salesmen, craftsmen, and service workers. Although not statistically significant, the distribution illustrates that the mobiles tend to have higher occupational aspirations for their sons.

One final measure served as an indicator of social class position. Respondents were asked to estimate their own social class position. The results are shown in Table 15. Most of the mothers estimated themselves to be working class. However, a slightly greater proportion of mobiles estimated themselves to be middle class. One must note, however, that

TABLE 14

PERCENTAGE DISTRIBUTION OF MOTHERS' OCCUPATIONAL ASPIRATIONS FOR THEIR SONS BY SUBSYSTEM

Occupational Desires*	Traditional (21) %	Deviant (13) %	Mobile (23) %
Professional, Proprietary, and Managerial	.48	.54	.78
Clerical, Sales, Crafts, and Service Workers	.52	.46	.22

$$x^2 = 4.76 \quad < .10 \text{ n.s.}$$

*A number of miscellaneous items were given as "none", "up to son", etc. and were equally distributed.

TABLE 15

PERCENTAGE DISTRIBUTION OF ESTIMATES OF SOCIAL CLASS POSITION AS REPORTED BY MOTHERS, BY SUBSYSTEM

Class Estimate	Traditional (22) %	Deviant (18) %	Mobile (26) %
Middle Class	.32	.44	.50
Working Class	.68	.56	.50

$$x^2 = 1.65 \text{ n.s.}$$

these differences were slight and not statistically significant.

Kinship Ties

Operational distinctions between expanded (traditional subsystem) and nuclear (mobile subsystem) family types would lead one to expect that expanded families would be larger than the nuclear both within the conjugal family unit and in terms of all available relatives. It was found that families of existing boys averaged 3.16 children per family while families of achieving boys averaged 2.88 children per family. This tends to support the hypotheses although the difference is slight. On the other hand, the size of the mixed family types (deviant subsystem) was the largest averaging 4.52 children (X^2 = 10.42 < .01 with 2 d.f.).

Of much more significance in terms of this study was the great disparity in number of relatives within the different families. Respondants were asked to list all living relatives whether of the family of orientation or procreation. Expanded families had the largest number of living relatives averaging 51.84 per family. In contrast, the nuclear family mothers reported an average of 34.84; and the mixed family mothers reported an average of 31.00.

Mothers were also asked to differentiate their relatives according to the degree of intimacy which existed. Four degrees of intimacy were designated as intimate, effective, non-effective, and unfamiliar. It was anticipated that relationships among relatives would be closer among expanded families generally. Nuclear families would be expected to have close ties which would be confined more to immediate family members. The mixed families would have lesser numbers of such ties both within the family and among the various relations.

In general, the relationships with all available relatives, beyond the immediate family, were found to be closer and more extensive within the traditional subsystem (expanded families) as compared to the other two. The deviant subsystem had the least number of intimate and effective ties and the highest number of unfamiliar. Table 16 shows these data.

TABLE 16

AVERAGE NUMBER OF LIVING RELATIVES BY DEGREE OF
INTIMACY OF RELATIONS AS REPORTED BY MOTHERS
BY SUBSYSTEM

Nature of Relationship	Family of Orientation			Family of Procreation		
	Traditional (24)	Deviant (18)	Mobile (26)	Traditional (24)	Deviant (18)	Mobile (26)
Intimate	12.15	4.95	6.45	3.85	.25	3.35
Effective	7.15	4.40	4.04	8.60	2.45	6.05
Non-effective	3.85	2.20	2.65	3.40	3.85	4.15
Unfamiliar	.62	2.27	1.77	1.35	1.90	.35

Comparisons which were made regarding the fathers' reports were similar to those of the mothers' and therefore support the contention that the families in the traditional subsystem were expanded in the sense that kinship ties were closer and more extensive compared to the mobile and deviant subsystems. This is shown in Table 17.

The data regarding the quality of relationships among relatives

TABLE 17

AVERAGE NUMBER OF LIVING RELATIVES BY DEGREE OF
INTIMACY OF RELATIONS AS REPORTED BY FATHERS
BY SUBSYSTEM

Nature of Relationship	Family of Orientation			Family of Procreation		
	Traditional (14)	Deviant (9)	Mobile (14)	Traditional (14)	Deviant (9)	Mobile (14)
Intimate	8.72	1.34	3.00	4.45	1.75	2.30
Effective	7.29	2.45	3.72	9.40	3.00	2.30
Non-affective	4.79	2.45	5.89	3.00	3.55	3.05
Unfamiliar	1.93	3.00	.85	3.70	.25	.15

was also organized in another way which more dramatically demonstrates
that families in the traditional subsystem have more extensive ties
which are closer when compared to the deviant and mobile subsystems.
Combining both the family of orientation and procreation (but excluding
the immediate family of the husband, wife, and children) the total number of relatives was tabulated. Relations which were described as
"close" (intimate and effective) were combined and compared with those
that were more "distant" (non-effective and unfamiliar). Table 18 shows
the responses of both mothers and fathers.

It is clear from Table 18 that the traditional subsystem respondants have closer and more extensive relations approximating the expanded family type as it was defined. Fifty-two per cent have 30 or more
intimate and effective ties as compared to only 35 per cent of the mobile and only 11 per cent of the deviant. This was found to be significant (X^2 = 7.86 < .025). On the other hand, the situation was reversed when more distant relations were compared. Seventy-eight per
cent of the deviants have six or more relatives that were noneffective
or unfamiliar compared with 73 per cent of the mobiles but only 48 per
cent of the traditionals. This was found to approach significance
(X^2 = 5.22 -- .10 level only). Although the sample was small, comparisons of fathers revealed similar kinds of relations.

To determine the degree of intimacy of parents within their own respective family of orientation, the number of family members (father,
mother, brother, and sister only) who were reported as being intimate
were tabulated in proportion to those who were not described as intimate. The combined responses of mothers and fathers revealed that 67
per cent of the traditionals were intimate compared to 58 per cent of
the mobiles, and 31 per cent of the deviants. Although this demonstrated the greater intimacy among expanded families in the traditional
subsystem, it also revealed that the nuclear families in the mobile
subsystem were less intimate in comparison. This was contrary to the
expectation that nuclear types would have closer ties within the conjugal family unit. The smaller number of mixed families having "intimate" ties is, however, quite obvious and consistent with the hypothe-

TABLE 18

PERCENTAGE DISTRIBUTION OF PARENTS ACCORDING TO THE
NUMBER AND KINDS OF RELATIONS WITH RELATIVES
BEYOND THE CONJUGAL FAMILY UNIT BY SUBSYSTEM

Number of Relatives	Mothers			Fathers*		
	Traditional (25)	Deviant (18)	Mobile (26)	Traditional (13)	Deviant (13)	Mobile (14)
Close: Intimate and Effective						
Under 30	.48	.89	.65	.62	1.00	.88
30 and Over	.52	.11	.35	.38	.00	.22
$x^2 = 7.86 < .025$						
Distant: Non-effective and Unfamiliar						
Under 6	.52	.22	.27	.38	.15	.43
6 and Over	.48	.78	.73	.62	.85	.57
$x^2 = 5.22 < .10$ n.s.						

*Tests of x^2 were not computed because of the smaller number of fathers.

ses. Table 19 summarizes these findings.

One final indicator of kinship ties was reflected in the comparison of relatives who lived in the neighborhood. According to the mothers interviewed, the traditionals averaged 5.17 relatives per family who were living in the neighborhood. The mobiles averaged 3.20 relatives per family and the deviants averaged 1.85 relatives per family.

TABLE 19

PROPORTIONS OF FAMILY OF ORIENTATION RELATIVES DESIGNATED BY PARENTS
TO BE "INTIMATE" AND "NON-INTIMATE" BY SUBSYSTEM

Nature of Relationship	Mothers			Fathers			Combined		
	Trad. (114)	Dev. (71)	Mob. (117)	Trad. (66)	Dev. (33)	Mob. (71)	Trad. (180)	Dev. (104)	Mob. (188)
Intimate	.73	.38	.58	.56	.15	.42	.67	.31	.58
Non-intimate	.27	.62	.42	.44	.85	.58	.33	.59	.43
	$x^2 = 21.93 < .005$			$x^2 = 15.09 < .005$			$x^2 = 36.24 < .005$		

This indicates a tendency on the part of the traditional families to remain together -- an attribute consistent with expectations for expanded families. Although the differences were not as great among the fathers, comparisons revealed the same tendencies.

Family Functioning

A number of measures were used to make some assessment of family functioning. Of particular interest was the question of how inclusive the family was regarding family affairs. Mutual help patterns and decision-making characteristics were also examined.

Eleven family gatherings were compared to get some indication of the degree of involvement of relatives in family activities.[1] A four-point scale was developed to reflect four levels of inclusiveness: (1) part of the family; (2) the entire family; (3) family and intimate relatives only; and (4) all available relatives. An index of family gatherings was computed by rating each family gathering from one to four accordingly; and, then using the sum as the final score. A total score of 44 (all available relatives at all eleven events) was taken to indicate the greatest expanded family score. Again, taking the mothers' responses as indicators of the family unit, Table 20 reveals how the traditional subsystem most nearly portrays the expanded family types. The traditional subsystem had a mean score of 31.85 in contrast to the means of 25.80 for the mobile subsystem and 22.28 for the deviant subsystem. The deviants generally had more family events which included only part of the family which suggests less family unity.

TABLE 20

PERCENTAGE DISTRIBUTION OF MOTHERS' SCORES
INDICATING THE DEGREE OF INCLUSION OF
RELATIVES IN ELEVEN FAMILY GATHERINGS
BY SUBSYSTEM

Scores Indicating Number of Relatives Included	Traditional (24) %	Deviant (18) %	Mobile (26) %
Under 30.00	.38	.83	.77
30.00 and over	.62	.17	.23
$x^2 = 12.21$ $< .005$			

It will be recalled that another major distinguishing characteristic which differentiates the expanded family type from the nuclear and mixed types is the emphasis on mutual help and association in contrast to more independence and isolated functioning. Operationally defined, the expanded family type will offer greater mutual help patterns for family members in such areas as finances, care of children, decision-making at times of illness and death, and a variety of other areas. These were expected to be less dominant among nuclear families and least dominant among the mixed families.

Four areas in which mutual help could be extended to relatives were examined: general aid, finances, care of children, and personal problems. Respondants were asked to indicate how frequently they gave such help -- offten, sometimes, or never. Responses in relation to all four areas were totaled and are presented in the frequency distribution in Table 21. The greater tendency of the traditionals to give help "often" is quite clear. Conversely, the greater tendency of the deviants to "never" give such help is also quite clear.

TABLE 21

FREQUENCY DISTRIBUTION OF HELP GIVEN TO RELATIVES BY
MOTHERS REGARDING FOUR SELECTIVELY COMBINED AREAS:
GENERAL AID, FINANCES, CARE OF CHILDREN, AND PERSONAL
PROBLEMS, BY SUBSYSTEM

Frequency of Help Given	Traditional (95)	Deviant (69)	Mobile (98)
Often	19	4	8
Sometimes	57	34	69
Never	19	31	21

$$x^2 = 22.61 \quad < .005$$

Mutual help patterns were also viewed in terms of the sources of help received which were categorized as follows: family, relatives, friends, or professionals. Frequencies of help received in times of trouble, with finances, care of children, and with personal problems, as presented in Table 22, reveal that the mobile subsystem received more help from the family. This supports the contention that the nuclear family predominates. On the other hand, relatives were good sources of help for both the traditional and mobile subsystems. The disparity in help received from friends is to be noted as the traditionals significantly received more help from this source.

Giving help to friends was also measured. Table 23 presents the frequency distribution of such help combining the areas of general aid, finances, care of children, and personal problems. Although this measure did not bear directly on comparing family types, it does suggest that the traditional subsystem tends to have mutual help patterns not only among relatives but with friends as well. Lesser numbers of mobile and deviant mothers mentioned "always" and otherwise indicated that they

60

TABLE 22

FREQUENCY DISTRIBUTION INDICATING SOURCES OF HELP
RECEIVED REGARDING FOUR SELECTIVELY COMBINED
AREAS: TIMES OF TROUBLE, FINANCES, CARE OF
CHILDREN, AND PERSONAL PROBLEMS, BY
SUBSYSTEM

Sources of Help Given	Traditional (87)	Deviant (61)	Mobile (107)
Family	26	24	44
Relatives	30	15	38
Friends	13	4	4
Professionals, etc.	18	18	21

$$x^2 = 12.80 \quad < .05$$

TABLE 23

FREQUENCY DISTRIBUTION OF HELP GIVEN TO FRIENDS BY
MOTHERS REGARDING FOUR SELECTIVELY COMBINED AREAS:
GENERAL AID, FINANCES, CARE OF CHILDREN, AND
PERSONAL PROBLEMS, BY SUBSYSTEM

Degree of Help Given	Traditional (90)	Deviant (64)	Mobile (89)
Always	13	4	3
Sometimes	50	32	52
Never	27	28	34

$$x^2 = 9.59 \quad < .05$$

helped friends less often.

Community and Neighborhood Contacts

As it was operationally defined, expanded families would be expected to be most identified with the neighborhood, while the nuclear and

61

mixed families would be expected to have more identification outside the neighborhood.

It has already been reported that among those fourteen families that moved from the neighborhood during the study period only one was from the traditional subsystem. When parents were asked to indicate how they viewed themselves in respect to the neighborhood, it was found that the traditional subsystem mothers stated that they felt they were like most of the others in the neighborhood in every single case. On the other hand, 11 per cent of the deviant and 19 per cent of the mobile stated that they felt like a certain segment or were "different from most." The distributions were not found to be statistically significant, however (X^2 = 5.15 $<$ .10 at 2 d.f.). Nevertheless, the responses do suggest that the traditionals more than the mobiles and deviants tend to feel they belong and are a part of the neighborhood.

Comparisons were also made to determine residence of friends to see if there were any perceptible differences which might indicate the degree to which persons maintained ties within or without the neighborhood. It was found that no statistically significant differences existed. Traditional mothers averaged 3.40 friends living in the neighborhood, deviant mothers averaged 3.41, and mobile mothers averaged 3.14. Also a look at how many friends were mentioned who lived outside of the neighborhood did not reveal statistically significant differences. It should be noted, however, that more mobile mothers (.36) had friends living outside the neighborhood as compared to the traditional (.25) and deviant (.17) mothers.

It was also possible to trace some of the friendships among the parents in the study to see to what extent they tended to select as friends other parents whose sons held similar value orientations. Although there was a considerable loss in number of cases because it was not possible to categorize many of the friends listed; it should be noted that the traditional parents showed a marked tendency to select other traditional parents as friends more often. Table 24 reveals how thirteen of twenty traditional subsystem selections that could be traced were traditional; four were mobile, and three were deviant. Five

TABLE 24

FREQUENCY DISTRIBUTION OF PARENTS' FRIENDSHIP
CHOICES MADE AND RECEIVED, BY SUBSYSTEM

Choices Made		Choices Received		
Number of Parents	Subsystem	Traditional (21)	Deviant (4)	Mobile (8)
(13)	Traditionals	13	3	4
(5)	Deviants	5	1	0
(3)	Mobiles	3	0	4

out of six deviant subsystem selections that could be traced were also traditional. Three out of seven mobile selections that could be traced were traditional; four were mobile. The number of cases is extremely small and not very trustworthy. To the extent that the greater popularity of the traditionals may serve as a crude indicator of their more central role in the neighborhood, those selecting traditionals may be demonstrating a greater identification.

Another crude indicator of identification was reflected in the question asked concerning desires for a high school in the neighborhood. Most felt there should be a high school. Greater proportions of the deviants (.95) and traditionals (.92) said the neighborhood needed a high school compared to mobiles (.73). This was not statistically significant however.

Another measure of identification with the neighborhood was reflected in the respondents' choice of neighborhood leaders and how close they were to them. The reasons for selecting "key" persons was analyzed to see which criteria served most often to differentiate the subsystem choices. The analysis revealed that in particular three criteria were more often mentioned as important: church affiliation, settlement house affiliation, and informal neighborhood contacts. Table 25 shows the percentage distribution found. More of the mobiles (.65) indicated that church affiliation was important in contrast to the traditionals (.46) and deviants (.39). More of the deviants (.61) indicated that the settlement house affiliations were important in contrast to the traditionals (.50) and the mobiles (.46). The traditional parents more often indicated that informal neighborhood contacts were important. The proportions were relatively small, however, with the traditionals having less than one-third (.29) in contrast to the mobiles (.16) and deviants (.11). In this regard, an unusually large number of traditional fathers (.43) indicated that informal neighborhood ties were important while more of the deviants and only a small number of mobile fathers (.14) saw informal neighborhood contacts to be important.

In addition, a formula was developed to see to what degree persons felt that they maintained relationships with the key persons mentioned. A score was given each person by assigning a numerical value to responses which showed the degree of relationship the respondent indicated existed between himself and each key person he noted. Scores ranged from zero to 4.00 representing a continuum from no relationship to a close one. The findings revealed that slightly more mobiles (Mean = 2.00) stated that they were closer to key persons. Traditional persons were less close (Mean = 1.77) and the deviants were the least (Mean = 1.26). These differences were not found to be statistically significant.

An analysis of formal associations disclosed that more traditional and mobile mothers belonged to formal associations. Using a simple scoring system weighting the nature of the involvement with associations, scores took account of attendance, offices held, committee membership, and financial contributions. Scores ranged from zero to 41 representing a continuum of no involvement to much involvement. The frequency distribution of the scores revealed that the deviants had the least involvement in formal associations. This is illustrated in Table 26.

From the foregoing, it may be concluded that there was little evidence to support the contention that there were appreciable differences

TABLE 25

PERCENTAGE DISTRIBUTION OF MOTHERS AND FATHERS LISTING
CHURCH, SETTLEMENT HOUSE, AND INFORMAL RELATIONSHIPS
AS CRITERIA FOR CHOOSING KEY NEIGHBORHOOD LEADERS,
BY SUBSYSTEM

Criteria*	Mothers			Fathers		
	Traditional (24) %	Deviant (18) %	Mobile (26) %	Traditional (14) %	Deviant (9) %	Mobile (14) %
Church	.46	.39	.65	.43	.11	.50
Settlement	.50	.61	.46	.50	.33	.43
Informal Relationships	.29	.11	.16	.43	.00	.14

*Other less often selected reasons given for selecting key neighborhood leaders were related to business, politics, neighborhood schools; and were fairly equally distributed.

TABLE 26

PERCENTAGE DISTRIBUTION OF MOTHERS' SCORES REVEALING
THE DEGREE OF INVOLVEMENT IN FORMAL ASSOCIATIONS
BY SUBSYSTEM

Scores	Traditional (23) %	Deviant (16) %	Mobile (25) %
Under 10.0	.43	.87	.64
11.0 and over	.57	.13	.36

between the subsystems in terms of their ties to the neighborhood. This is somewhat obscured by the fact that all three family types showed a high degree of identification with the neighborhood generally. The data failed to differentiate persons accordingly, although in a rough and sometimes indirect manner the direction of the distributions were in the

64

hypothesized direction.

In this connection, the expanded families in the traditional sub-system more often felt themselves to be like others in the neighborhood; they had more friends who were known to be traditionals; they felt strongly about the need for a neighborhood high school; saw informal neighborhood contacts to be of importance to leaders; and were more involved in formal associations. The nuclear families more often saw themselves as different from "most others" in the neighborhood; they had more friends living outside the neighborhood; they were closer, however, to the neighborhood leaders; and quite involved in formal associations. Although the mixed families felt the strongest about needing a neighborhood high school, they were least related to neighborhood leaders, and were the least involved in formal associations.

The findings regarding family types appear to fit the operational definitions as originally provided. The expanded family tended to typify the stable working class in terms of family income, aspirations, and the like. Kinship ties were closer and more demanding with regard to mutual assistance and involvement in family affairs. There was also a trend towards greater identification with the neighborhood. The mixed family type was typified by its extreme contrasts. In terms of social class it had the least financial resources and the lowest levels of aspirations. Kinship ties were most distant, and least demanding regarding mutual assistance and involvement in family affairs. Participation in the community and neighborhood reflected the least identification with the neighborhood. And finally, the nuclear family type was characteristically middle class, having larger family incomes and higher aspirations. Relative to the other family types, kinship ties were not as extensive or as intensive as the expanded family type, nor were they as limited or distant as the mixed family type. The nature of the nuclear family's engagement in the community and neighborhood suggested a meaningful involvement.

Group Associations

Information regarding group associations and group properties was gathered from two principle sources. The Describe Your Group Questionnaire was used to elicit the boys' own reports concerning their group preferences and associations and represented their perceptions regarding groups. A second, more objective measure was made possible through the use of previously kept agency attendance rosters on all kinds of peer groups. Such records were utilized as they applied to the boys in the study. This was found to be a good source of information concerning boys' actual behavior relevant to peer groups.

The material in this section is organized to reflect the group properties as they are spelled out in the hypotheses regarding corner-boy, deviant-boy, and college-boy groups. These properties include group size, open or closed membership patterns, degree of engagement in the group, and group cohesiveness.

Group Size

When boys were asked to describe their own group it was found that the group size varied slightly by subsystem. Deviant boys tended to be members of larger groups which was hypothesized for deviant-boy groups. Deviant boys reported an average of 6.11 members per group while the traditionals averaged 5.92 and the mobiles averaged 5.44.

Boys' preferences regarding the size of the ideal group showed a similar tendency of the deviants to prefer larger groups although again the findings were not statistically significant. The greater preference for smaller groups on the part of the traditional and mobile subsystems is also evident. Table 27 shows the proportionate distribution of the boys' preferences regarding group size.

TABLE 27

PERCENTAGE DISTRIBUTION OF BOYS' PREFERENCES REGARDING
GROUP SIZE BY SUBSYSTEM

Group Size Preferred	Traditional (25) %	Deviant (27) %	Mobile (27) %
Six and Under	.48	.37	.52
Seven to Eleven	.48	.41	.44
Twelve and Over	.04	.22	.04

$$x^2 = 6.78 \text{ n.s.}$$

A review of agency records concerning boys' memberships in agency sponsored groups was used in comparing boys' actual behavior regarding group size. Agency rosters, reporting on 51 groups over a six-year period, were analyzed. Each member who had been categorized by value orientation was examined in relation to his group memberships. About two-thirds of all memberships in the 51 groups were identified and therefore served as the basis for subsequent comparisons of the boys.

In addition to a comparison of number of memberships, percent attendance of each boy was computed and averaged with other boys holding similar value orientations in the same group. This measure was used as an indicator of involvement in the group. This was necessary to assess individual participation to determine if the membership in the group was active. Table 28 shows the comparison of boys according to the number of memberships which were found in the agency groups by group size. The tendency of the mobiles to have more memberships in smaller groups is clear. The deviants tend to have more memberships in larger groups although it should also be noted that they have more memberships in smaller groups as well. Percentage differences in attendance reveals that the traditionals (70.6) and the mobiles (69.4) were higher than the deviants (58.2) in small group memberships. But the situation is reversed with respect to larger groups where the deviants (67.2) are more active than the mobiles (54.3) and the traditionals (50.9).

TABLE 28

NUMBER OF MEMBERSHIPS AND PER CENT ATTENDANCE OF
BOYS IN FIFTY-ONE ORGANIZED GROUPS DISTRIBUTED
BY GROUP SIZE AND BY SUBSYSTEM

Group Size	Traditional (77)		Deviant (124)		Mobile (59)	
	Member-ships	Per Cent Attend-ance	Member-ships	Per Cent Attend-ance	Member-ships	Per Cent Attend-ance
Four to Twelve	34	70.6	50	58.2	35	69.4
Thirteen to Twenty	25	59.2	34	56.3	11	27.2
Twenty and Over	18	50.9	40	67.2	13	54.3

$$x^2 = 7.56 \text{ n.s.} \quad 4 \text{ d.f.}$$

The data presented concerning the size of groups merely indicate certain tendencies on the part of the deviant boys to belong to deviant-boy groups in the sense that they are larger. The tendencies of the mobile boys and traditional boys to belong to smaller groups are also apparent. However, the findings were not determined to be statistically significant and therefore no definite conclusions can be reached.

Open or Closed Membership Patterns

A number of measures were utilized to give a picture of membership patterns as to whether they were open or closed in nature. One such measure was inferred from the tendency of the groups to have other boys or non-members associating with the group members generally. It was found that the actual number of "other boys" who were designated as associating with the group, but who were not regular members, was largest among the deviant boys, with a mean of 5.67 boys mentioned per boy. The mobile boys averaged 4.44 and the traditionals had the least with a mean of 3.04.

Table 29 graphically demonstrates the tendency on the part of the deviant boys to have more "other boys" which is indicative of the openness of their groups, and which is consistent with the deviant-boy group as defined. At the same time, the higher proportion of traditional boys who reported smaller numbers of other boys associating with their groups implies a more closed grouping pattern which is consistent with the corner-boy group as defined. It should be noted that although this factor can serve as an indicator of the groups' openness, strictly speaking, this does not represent the degree to which these non-members are permitted entry into the group.

Another measure was available which showed how many newcomers or outsiders were permitted to become members of groups. Boys were asked to indicate if their group had any recent new members. The deviants had the highest proportion (.26), stating that their group had recently acquired new members. These data are shown in Table 30.

TABLE 29

PERCENTAGE DISTRIBUTION OF THE NON-MEMBERS ASSOCIATING
WITH BOYS' GROUPS AS REPORTED BY BOYS, BY SUBSYSTEM

Number of "Other" Boys Associated with Groups	Traditional (25) %	Deviant (27) %	Mobile (27) %
Under Two	.48	.22	.33
Three to Five	.48	.45	.48
Six and Over	.04	.33	.19

$$x^2 = 8.47 \quad < \quad .10 \text{ n.s.}$$

TABLE 30

PERCENTAGE DISTRIBUTION OF BOYS INDICATING THEIR GROUP
HAD RECENTLY ACQUIRED NEW MEMBERS, BY SUBSYSTEM

New Members	Traditional (25) %	Deviant (27) %	Mobile (27) %
No New Members	.96	.74	.93
New Members	.04	.26	.07

$$x^2 = 6.67 \quad < .05$$

A variety of other measures were used to determine how open the groups were to others. Boys were asked to give their preferences in this matter in three different ways: first, they were asked if in a team sport such as basketball they would welcome other players in the group; second, whether an ideal club should be open or closed to others;

and third, if an ideal club should be limited to only friends or should include others besides friends.

Regarding the basketball team, the traditionals had the greatest proportion (.72) desiring to keep the players confined to the group. Deviant boys (.59) and mobile boys (.56) had slightly lesser proportions. Larger proportions of the traditionals (.66) and deviants (.63) indicated that the ideal club should be closed to outsiders in contrast to a relatively low proportion (.37) of mobiles. With respect to whether the ideal club should include others besides friends, a very similar pattern was found. Greater proportions of deviants (.59) and traditionals (.56) felt that the club should be limited to only friends while a greater proportion of mobiles (.63) felt that the ideal club should include others besides friends. The three criteria have been combined in Table 31.

TABLE 31

PERCENTAGE DISTRIBUTION OF BOYS INDICATING THE IDEAL
GROUP TO BE OPEN OR CLOSED ACCORDING TO THREE
SELECTED CRITERIA: PLAYING ON A BASKETBALL
TEAM, RECEPTIVITY TO FRIENDS, AND RECEP-
TIVITY TO OTHERS, BY SUBSYSTEM

Preferences	Traditional (75) %	Deviant (91) %	Mobile (91) %
Preferences to be Open	.39	.39	.56
Preferences to be Closed	.61	.61	.44

$$x^2 = 6.75 \quad < .05$$

It can be seen that deviant and traditional boys both share preferences for closed groups. In respect to the deviant boys this is contrary to their actual experiences with newcomers and other boys as they reported. Furthermore, the deviant boys, contrary to expectation, more often stated that it was not easy to become a member of their groups. This is shown in Table 32.

Although the traditionals appear to consistently prefer and belong to closed rather than open groups which can be termed corner-boy groups; and, the mobile consistently prefer and belong to open rather than closed groups termed as college-boy groups; the descrepancy among the deviant appears to be contradicting. It was found that they belonged to groups that were more or less open but their preferences were for closed groups. Although this may suggest a certain wishful thinking on

TABLE 32

PERCENTAGE DISTRIBUTION OF BOYS INDICATING HOW EASY IT WAS TO BECOME A MEMBER OF THEIR GROUPS, BY SUBSYSTEM

Availability of Memberships	Traditional (25)	Deviant (27)	Mobile (27)
Easy to Become a Member	.48	.33	.78
Not Easy to Become a Member	.52	.67	.22

$$x^2 = 11.11 \quad < .005$$

the part of the deviant boys, age differences appear to have influenced the findings. For example, a higher percentage of deviant boys who stated that they preferred "open" groups were under fifteen years of age, while a smaller percentage of traditionals and mobiles under the age of fifteen preferred open groups.

Closely related to the question of how open or closed the groups were, is the question of how many varied memberships boys had in groups. Operationally defined, members of open groups might also be expected to belong to more groups while members of closed groups might tend to belong to only a few.

Agency records were used to determine the number of group memberships each boy was known to have in agency formed groups. While this was a crude measure not taking into account a variety of other group associations, it does indicate there is a significant difference of known memberships among boys. This was useful in comparing boys.

Table 33 shows a higher proportion of deviant boys who belonged to over three groups as compared to the traditionals and mobiles. The mobile boys, on the other hand, were members of less groups.

While this shows a higher number of group memberships for deviants, the exceptionally low number for mobile boys must be explained. Twenty of the mobile boys had no memberships at all according to the records. These findings refer only to the known memberships in the settlement house and obviously other memberships do exist which have not been documented here.

Boys were also asked to express their opinions as to whether boys should be members of many, a few, or only one group. In this regard, the deviants' preference for many groups and the traditionals' preference for only one group are clear, although this was not statistically significant.

TABLE 33

THE PROPORTION OF MEMBERSHIPS EACH BOY HAD IN AGENCY
SPONSORED GROUPS OVER A FIVE YEAR PERIOD, BY
SUBSYSTEM

Number of Group Memberships	Traditional (27)	Deviant (32)	Mobile (38)
Three and Under	.70	.50	.84
Over Three	.30	.50	.16

$$x^2 = 9.55 \quad < .01$$

TABLE 34

THE PROPORTION OF BOYS' PREFERENCES REGARDING SINGLE
OR MULTIPLE GROUP MEMBERSHIPS, BY SUBSYSTEM

Number of Groups of Which Boys Should be Members	Traditional (25)	Deviant (27)	Mobile (27)
Only of One Group	.72	.48	.52
More than One Group	.28	.52	.48

$$x^2 = 3.45 \text{ n.s.}$$

Degree of Engagement in the Group

According to the definitions provided, members of corner-boy groups
would reflect a greater engagement or involvement in their groups, in
that the groups would involve their members more often and totally in
group activities. In contrast, the college-boy group (mobile subsystem)
would be together least often and involve members in more segmented
ways. The deviant-boy group would in all likelihood involve its members most often in its activities; but, because of its "openness", it
would not always require full attendance.

Table 35 depicts the distribution of boys' memberships in fifty-one
different groups organized as part of the settlement program. A comparison of per cent attendance by the nature of the activity will give
some indication of differential engagement in groups. The greater involvement of the traditionals in club activity (.73) is apparent. Although the actual numbers are small, the greater per cent attendance of

71

TABLE 35

DISTRIBUTION OF MEMBERSHIPS AND PER CENT ATTENDANCE OF
BOYS IN FIFTY-ONE ORGANIZED GROUPS ACCORDING TO GROUP
ACTIVITY AND SUBSYSTEM

Group Activities		Traditional		Deviant		Mobile	
Kind of Group	No. of Groups (51)	Member-ships	Per Cent Attendance	Member-ships	Per Cent Attendance	Member-ships	Per Cent Attendance
Clubs	(24)	35	.73	45	.65	28	.66
Councils	(1)	1	.50	0	.00	2	.66
Class-Gym	(7)	18	.57	23	.60	11	.52
Class-Swim	(8)	10	.51	15	.49	8	.43
Class-Craft	(4)	2	.43	4	.35	5	.69
Canteen	(7)	10	.46	36	.69	6	.45

mobiles in "council" (.66) and crafts (.69) is consistent with expectations. The greater involvement of deviants in canteen (.69) is also consistent with the prediction that these boys tend to participate in larger, less "close-knit" group associations.

In the Describe Your Group Questionnaire boys were asked to indicate how frequently part or all of their groups participated in ten different activities. The possible responses -- always, often, sometimes, seldom, and never -- were given point values from four to zero. These were totaled and used as a score indicating how frequently any given boy participated with his group in these ten activities. Possible scores ranged from zero to forty. The findings revealed very slight differences and were not significant. This is shown in Table 36.

TABLE 36

PERCENTAGE DISTRIBUTION OF BOYS' SCORES AS AN INDEX
OF FREQUENCY PARTICIPATION OF BOYS IN TEN SELECTED
ACTIVITIES, BY SUBSYSTEM

Scores Indicating Frequency Participation	Traditional (25) %	Deviant (27) %	Mobile (27) %
0 to 24	.64	.70	.74
25 and Over	.36	.30	.26
x^2 = 2.49 n.s.			

An analysis of responses was also made to determine whether part or most group members were typically together while participating in these activities. In particular, seven areas were used, eliminating spectator activities such as watching sports, going to movies, and watching television. This was done because all of these tended to involve only some members and seldom included most of the groups. All of the other responses were totaled and compared to see how many times all members were included. Table 37 shows the results.

The greater tendency on the part of the mobiles to include only part of the group (.62) stands in contrast to the deviants who tend to include most members (.54). Slightly more traditionals (.58) included only part of the group and in this sense were not as engaging as was anticipated.

A more detailed look at the distributions relative to each specific activity gave some indication of the kinds of group activities valued by the boys. Table 38 shows the proportion of boys indicating their group participated in the activity "always" or "often".

73

TABLE 37

PERCENTAGE DISTRIBUTION OF BOYS' INVOLVEMENT IN GROUPS
WITHIN SEVEN SELECTED GROUP ACTIVITIES: SCHOOL,
SETTLEMENT HOUSE, SPORTS, HANGING AROUND, DRIVING
AROUND, ATTENDING PARTIES, ATTENDING SPECIAL
EVENTS, BY SUBSYSTEM

Degree of Group Involvement	Traditional (140) %	Deviant (158) %	Mobile (157) %
Part of the Group	.58	.46	.62
Most All of the Group	.42	.54	.38

$$x^2 = 8.31 \quad < .025$$

TABLE 38

COMPARISONS OF PROPORTIONS OF BOYS WHO INDICATED
FREQUENT GROUP PARTICIPATION ACCORDING TO TEN
GROUP ACTIVITIES, BY SUBSYSTEM

Group Activity	Traditional (25)		Deviant (27)		Mobile (27)	
	%	Rank	%	Rank*	%	Rank
School	.44	4	.33	8	.48	3
Settlement House	.60	2.5	.41	6.5	.37	7
Playing Sports	.60	2.5	.53	2	.63	2
Watching Sports	.32	6	.30	9	.41	6
Going to Movies	.32	6	.41	6.5	.44	4.5
Watching Television	.16	10	.22	10	.19	10
Hanging Around	.80	1	.90	1	.85	1
Driving Around	.28	8	.48	4	.30	8
Attending Parties	.24	9	.44	5	.26	9
Holidays and Special Events	.32	6	.52	3	.44	4.5

*It should be noted that while differences in ranking are small, the deviants' high rank for "driving around" and lower rank for "school" reflect their age and circumstances.

Other questions which were designed to ascertain certain facts regarding the degree to which the group requires total or partial involvement did not reveal any significant differences. In some cases,

74

such as the dilemma pitting the group against the home responsibilities, and going with the group in preference to going for a ride with older boys; the traditional boys had greater proportions of responses favoring the group. In pitting the group against friendships, or against taking a part-time job, the deviants had slightly higher preferences for the group.

Group Cohesion

According to the hypotheses, traditional boys will belong to corner-boy groups which will be more cohesive and closely-knit being less tolerant of cliques and isolates. In comparison, deviant boys will belong to deviant-boy groups which will be characterized by less cohesive ties and more tolerance of cliques and isolates.

An attempt was made to measure cohesiveness along a variety of dimensions -- friendship ties, desiring the same things, high prestige, sharing, sticking together, feeling the same way about things, and satisfactions with the group. Generally, although they were in the hypothesized direction, only slight differences were found in terms of these sources of cohesion.

One rather crude and indirect indicator of cohesion was a measure of the relative visibility of groups. This was the boys' perceptions of how easy it was to tell who were group members. On the theory that such a perception would show how much the boys regarded the group as a separate identifiable entity, this could reflect some aspect of the group's cohesive qualities. Table 39 gives the proportionate distribution of responses to the question of group visibility. According to the boys' perceptions, the traditionals and deviants tend to see their groups as standing out while almost one-half of the mobile boys regard their group as inconspicuous.

TABLE 39

PERCENTAGE DISTRIBUTION OF BOYS INDICATING THE VISIBILITY
OF THEIR GROUP MEMBERSHIP, BY SUBSYSTEM

Degree of Visibility of Group	Traditional (25) %	Deviant (27) %	Mobile (27) %
Easy to Tell Who Are Members	.88	.74	.53
Not Easy to Tell Who Are Members	.12	.26	.48

$$x^2 = 8.42 \quad < .025$$

A more direct measure of cohesion was possible in a detailed analysis by first taking friendship and then taking membership choices in assessing mutual acceptance patterns which would reflect degrees of cohesion. Sociograms were employed to trace all known friendship and membership selections separately. The degree of inter-selectivity among the boys in the same friendship or membership group was then measured by means of a formula devised specifically for this purpose. A per cent of internal selection for each boy's group was computed by means of the following formula:

$$\frac{\leq \text{ Choices}}{N (N-1)}$$

The sum of the choices was the total number of selections of boys within the group by all who were designated to be in the group. N equalled the size of the group (in the friendship group this was usually four since boys were asked to name three friends; in the membership group this was one plus the number of boys designated by each boy).

Whenever a group member could not be identified in the sociogram, he was dropped from the group and the size of the group was reduced in the formula. A score of 1.00 would indicate that there was total inter-selectivity. Each boy originally identified would have had to name every other boy and be named by each of them in order to achieve this score. The proportionate distribution of scores which resulted by using this method of comparison to examine friendship choices is presented in Table 40.

TABLE 40

PERCENTAGE DISTRIBUTION OF BOYS' SCORES REFLECTING
INTER-FRIENDSHIP CHOICES WITHIN FRIENDSHIP GROUPS
BY SUBSYSTEM

Scores	Traditional (23) %	Deviant (26) %	Mobile (23) %
.51 to 1.00	.70	.35	.39
.01 to .50	.13	.35	.18
	$x^2 = 4.98 < .10$		
Zero*	.17	.30	.43

*A zero score was obtained whenever none of the boys in the group indicated by the respondant reciprocated or named another of the designated group. Less mobiles could be traced which in part accounts for their large (.43) proportion of zero scores.

Although it was not statistically significant, more inter-selectivity among friends was found among the traditionals indicating a closer-knit structure. On the other hand, the deviants had the lowest scores of all three. The mean scores were as follows: traditionals, 60.52; mobiles, 43.3; and deviants, 42.1.

In a similar kind of analysis, the amount of groupiness or close-knit characteristics of each boy's designated membership group was determined. The proportionate distribution of these scores are presented in Table 41. The means of these scores revealed a higher degree of inter-selectivity among the traditionals (67.0) as compared to the deviants (61.7) and mobiles (53.7).

TABLE 41

PERCENTAGE DISTRIBUTION OF BOYS' SCORES REFLECTING
INTER-MEMBERSHIP CHOICES WITHIN MEMBERSHIP GROUPS
BY SUBSYSTEM

Scores	Traditional (23)	Deviant (25)	Mobile (24)
.51 - 1.00	.83	.52	.62
.01 - .50	.08	.40	.17
$x^2 = 6.95 < .05$			
Zero	.08	.08	.21

A further comparison of the friendship group scores and the membership scores was made to see how friendship selections resembled membership selections in peer groups. A higher correlation was found among the traditional (Rho = .80). In contrast, the deviant scores from the two groups were the least correlated (Rho = .34). The mobile scores were moderately correlated (Rho = .52). Thus it can be concluded that friendship selections varied directly with membership selections among the traditionals (t test was determined to be 6.11 < .001). Among the mobiles there was also a statistically significant relationship between the two groups (t test was 2.79 < .02). But the deviants appeared to have inter-selectivity selections in the friendship and membership groups that were not significantly correlated (t test 1.76 < .10 n.s.). These findings would suggest that the membership groups of the traditional and mobile boys would more often reflect friendship selections and vice versa. The relationship of friendship and membership selections is less related among deviants.

Another way of measuring sociometric attraction was to compute the number of mutual choices made. In a sense this was an awareness measure of other "similarly inclined boys." More reciprocated friendships were present among the traditionals; while the least number were present among the deviants. Similarly, reciprocal membership choices disclosed the same differences. The data suggest therefore, that the traditional boys belong to deviant-boy groups which are less cohesive and close-knit. Table 42 shows the reciprocal friendship and membership choices.

TABLE 42

PERCENTAGE DISTRIBUTION OF BOYS' FRIENDSHIP AND
MEMBERSHIP GROUP CHOICES INDICATING MUTUAL AND
NON-RECIPROCAL SELECTIONS, BY SUBSYSTEM

Sociometric Choices	Traditional	Deviant	Mobile
Friendship Choices	(40)	(46)	(35)
Mutual Choices	.63	.30	.43
Not Reciprocated	.37	.70	.57
$x^2 = 8.96 < .025$			
Membership Choices	(78)	(87)	(60)
Mutual Choices	.59	.36	.50
Not Reciprocated	.41	.64	.50
$x^2 = 9.18 < .025$			

One final test was conducted which focused on the broader study of groups beyond the friendship or peer group to see to what extent the subsystem identification was related to interpersonal choices. Although the hypotheses refer to peer groups, it does appear likely that the selections and choices from subsystem to subsystem should also vary if the value orientation of the individual has certain correlates which can be related to group properties generally.

The total number of friendship and membership selections were tabulated to identify the initiator and receiver of each choice that was made. There is unmistakable evidence to show that the subsystems as they reflect the value orientations of the boys is related to friendship and membership patterns. The traditionals and deviants show the greatest tendencies to select from within their respective subsystem. The mobiles split largely between the traditionals and mobiles. It can be seen also that the affinity between the mobiles and deviants is small; while the greater general popularity of the traditionals is obvious. This is illustrated in Table 43.

The data concerning group types, with a few modifications, fit the descriptions for the corner-boy, deviant-boy, and college-boy groups as originally hypothesized. The corner-boy group was found to be small in size, and relatively closed in its membership characteristics. Although it was not "totally" engaging of its members, more often its members

TABLE 43

FREQUENCY DISTRIBUTION OF FRIENDSHIP AND MEMBERSHIP
CHOICES MADE AND RECEIVED, BY SUBSYSTEM

Choices Made		Choices Received		
		Traditional	Deviant	Mobile
Friendship Choices Made	Number of Boys	(40)	(46)	(35)
Traditional	(23)	21	13	18
Deviant	(26)	5	27	4
Mobile	(26)	14	6	13

$$x^2 = 30.19 < .005$$

Membership Choices Made				
		(78)	(87)	(60)
Traditional	(23)	34	27	28
Deviant	(26)	19	53	11
Mobile	(25)	25	7	21

$$x^2 = 39.84 < .005$$

were not usually members of other groups and the extremely cohesive, close-knit qualities were clearly evidenced. The deviant-boy group had both small and large groups, and appeared to be both closed and open in membership. Compared to the other types, there also was a greater degree of involvement and engagement of its members in group activities, although at the same time it most significantly lacked group cohesiveness in terms of mutual selections and attraction. And finally, the college-boy group was smaller in size than was anticipated, although it was more often open in membership. It was also found that members were least engaged or involved in group activities, and the groups were only moderately cohesive.

In summary, the findings reported in this chapter bear out the hypotheses that there are distinctive subsystems with characteristic values, family types, and group properties. Based on the individual value orientations of the boys, family types were discovered which revealed relative differences related to social class such as family income, occupational and educational aspirations, and the like. The size of the family in terms of number of relatives differed as did the intensity of relationships among them. The amount of help which was given to each other and to friends varied; and, relatives were differentially included in family affairs. Also, there were some indications that the degree of identification with the community and neighborhood differed. Group types were likewise found to differ in varying degrees in respect to group size, open versus closed membership patterns, degree of engagement in the group, and group cohesion.

FOOTNOTES--CHAPTER III

[1]The eleven family gatherings listed were: New Year's, Easter, Fourth of July, Feast of the Assumption, Thanksgiving, Christmas, Birthdays, Anniversaries, Christening and Communions, Weddings, and Funerals.   See Appendix D.

CHAPTER IV

INTERPRETATIONS AND IMPLICATIONS

Interpretation of the Findings

The purpose of this study was to determine to what extent boys with similar value orientations came from similar types of families and belonged to similar peer groups. Although initially, an entire neighborhood population of boys was included in the study, a sample was selected based on value differences among the boys. Comparisons of the boys, their parents, and their peers clearly demonstrated that there was a relationship among individual value orientations, family patterns, and peer group associations. Furthermore, these social variables were so related as to sufficiently distinguish the existence of at least three diverse subsystems reflecting predictably characteristic values, family types, and peer group properties.

The hypotheses were generally supported although the empirical evidence suggested modifications of certain variable attributes as they were operationally defined. In the main, there was a definite relationship of a boy's value orientation to his family type and to the nature of his peer group associations -- all three variables were seen to be facets of his subsystem identification in the neighborhood. More specifically, the hypotheses supported by the data were as follows: the traditional subsystem was made up of boys with existing value orientations who came from expanded families and belonged to corner-boy groups; the mobile subsystem was made up of boys with achieving value orientations who came from nuclear families and belonged to college-boy groups; and the deviant subsystem was made up of boys with conflicting value orientations who came from mixed families and belonged to deviant-boy groups.

Theory

The review of the literature on social stratification generally revealed that there were corresponding relationships between values, family life, and peer groups. Many community studies were also cited which documented class differences among people and demonstrated to greater or lesser degrees how these variables differ from class to class. For purposes of this study, these findings were explained in terms of a general functional theory which held that a person's values would bear some functional relationship to his family pattern and group associations.

In this theoretical context, the findings reported here support these views and acknowledge their usefulness as a general frame of reference for making comparative studies of neighborhoods. However, the findings also raised questions regarding the assumption that a neighborhood, where it reflects a particular social class level, can be treated as a relatively homogeneous unit. Such a conception has been

81

shown to be overly gross and misleading, and not very useful in terms of social work practice. Of greater utility was the finding that what appears to be a stable working-class neighborhood was in fact made up of distinctive subsystems displaying varying degrees of class-related attributes.

In other respects, the data strongly supports the work of Loomis whose theoretical perspective regarding the analysis of social systems was particularly relevant to the problem as formulated in this study. In keeping with the functional approach, this study stressed that social phenomena could not be studied effectively without corresponding attention to the functional interdependence of social units to each other and to the larger whole. In Loomis' conception, the internal aspects of any social system are so much a part of the larger external system that these can be studied in the same terms. The linkages that were predicted and found to be operative in respect to the variables generally show the utility of this conceptual formulation.

Although it was not clearly evident, inasmuch as it was not specifically tested in the study,[1] the subsystems similarly could be viewed as functionally related to each other and to the larger neighborhood whole. The existence of three clearly distinguishable subsystems with sufficiently different characteristics was well demonstrated in this study.

Broadly speaking, the findings support much of the previous work regarding values, families, and groups. The fact that there were extensive differences in value orientations among the boys as predicted supports the contention that the boys were validly discriminated in this regard. Value differences were consistent therefore with the descriptive typologies offered by Kluckhohn and Strodtbeck, Cohen, Clark and Wenninger, and Miller and Riessman whose concepts figured prominently in the measurements. The somewhat incidental observation regarding the greater range of "conflicting" values among deviant boys tentatively illustrated their lower commitment to any consistent value stance--which is generally recognized in theoretical formulations regarding deviant behavior.

Distinctions regarding nuclear and extended families and how they vary within the social class system were also generally supported in the data. Although previous empirical studies were sometimes found to be contradictory and lacking in clear-cut distinctions, the findings here clearly differentiated types of families within the sample. The findings obviously do not resolve the question debated by Parsons, Litwak and others regarding which type is most functional in modern society. One may conclude, however, that there may be an intervening variable such as revealed in subsystem identification wherein a functional analysis of the family may yield more consistent results.

The literature on the small group was found to be lacking in that theories had not been adequately developed to deal with social class influences on group properties. The groups described were conceived as ideal types and were drawn from the works of Whyte and Cohen. It should be clear, however, that in no way did this study attempt to compare anything more than certain specific group properties with reference to these group types. Nevertheless, the findings supported the view that groups served some functional usefulness for members as suggested, for example, by Cohen, Cloward and Ohlin, and other theorists who seek to explain the emergence of the delinquent subculture.

Individual Value Orientations

A review of the literature concerning social class values repeatedly demonstrated how values vary within the stratification system. Differences were found in aspirations, types of social relations established, and valuations concerning the use of time. In general, higher aspirations and achievement motivations were associated with middle-class persons who were characterized by their desire to get more education, seek suitable careers, and "get ahead." In contrast, the values of working-class persons place less emphasis on achievement and accomplishment in the middle-class sense of status and prestige. This could be attributed to the fact that working-class persons are more often caught up with the day-to-day problem of merely "getting by." Accordingly, they are found to be pragmatic and anti-intellectual in their outlook. In terms of relationships, the greater facility among the middle classes for moving in secondary group associations as responsible individuals, functioning in a manner prescribed by role-to-role expectations, stands in contrast to the tendency among the working classes to rely on the solidarity of the group, preferring intimate person-to-person relationships. And finally, the middle-class emphasis on constructive use of free time and preparation and planning for the future differs from the working-class day-to-day life style which is somewhat traditional in outlook and relatively uninfluenced by long-term future goals and objectives.

This study demonstrated how boys who presumably came from the same working-class origins, and lived in the same ethnic neighborhood, vary in their value orientations in a manner which parallels the wider social stratification system. To be sure, more boys were found to assimilate to some degree the middle-class value system reflecting the society as a whole. This finding is consistent with previous research as reported in the literature.[2] It appears to indicate the need for more refined instruments for measuring values, especially those which have been described as working-class in nature.

The "What Do You Think Questionnaire" was found to be generally useful for comparative purposes and in this sense served to differentiate boys according to their value orientations. The boys who favored achieving values and rejected the existing values were more clearly determined in this test and served to differentiate mobile (achieving) boys. On the other hand, the traditional boys, except in their preference for group solidarity, did not favor existing values over achieving values. But the preferences of the traditional boys for existing values were clear and obvious relative to the mobile boys. In two instances traditional boys preferred achieving values (i.e., a being philosophy and intellectualism) in greater proportions than the mobile boys. This raises serious questions regarding the discriminatory power of these two items. It is possible that the statements were not appropriately phrased. For example, the statement meant to elicit a doing philosophy was as follows: "The most important thing in life is to be able to do things well." The use of the phrase "do things well" may have been tapping desires for successful activity and, in this sense, the statement failed to highlight the distinction between doing and being. The statement which was meant to portray a preference for the intellectual was, "People with a lot of education give the best advice about life." In effect, such a statement might conceivably be reflecting an admiration for smartness[3] and know-how which could have obscured the academic and intellectual sense intended.

It was also useful to have information concerning values held by boys who were judged to be conflicting although this played no part in their designation in the study group. This was so because there was very little evidence in the literature to show that there were "delin-quent values," and also because it was hypothesized that so much of the deviant behavior was instrumentally devised to cope with negative soci-etal reactions and rejected status coming from the other two subsystems. This quality, incidently, may be reflected in the emphasis conflicting boys placed on role-to-role relationships -- which in a sense implies using oneself in a calculated way. On the other hand, the preferences of the deviants for person-to-person relationships were not consistent and again suggested mixed orientations. The strong sense of group soli-darity and the low emphasis on individual responsibility suggest that there may be a greater feeling of investment in the group as a way of potentially solving problems of adjustment. In another instance, the deviants' preference for planning use of free time was greater than either of the other two and may reflect a desire to leave the present situation for something more promising. Obviously, differences in pro-portions were not conclusive; and, these observations are only tenta-tive in that the data are viewed only as they may be consistent with the over-all concepts regarding the functioning of boys in respect to their value orientations.

Family Types

The literature clearly illustrates that family types vary accord-ing to social class levels and typically display differences which are related to regional, racial, and ethnic factors. The concept of the isolated nuclear family which has been associated with American society applies to the dominant middle class and is characterized by the inde-pendence, mobility, and strength of the conjugal unit. On the other hand, the working-class subculture appears to consist of families where meager economic resources and crisis situations, stemming from a more difficult day-to-day existence, tend to draw extended kin together for mutual assistance and support. Such families were found to be less mo-bile and self-sufficient as a conjugal unit.

This study revealed that there were similar differences found a-mong the boys' families in the sample. The mobiles (nuclear families) had, on the whole, greater resources reflected in larger family incomes and higher levels of aspirations for their children, less evidence of extended and intimate kinship ties, less involvement of extended kin in family affairs, and less occasions to extend and receive help from rela-tives. The traditionals (expanding families) on the other hand, had less resources reflecting more modest family incomes and lower aspira-tions, much more evidence of extended and intimate kinship ties, great-er involvement of relatives in family affairs, and more occasions to extend and receive help from relatives.

While these differences were documented and found to be statistic-ally significant, it was not shown how the conjugal unit itself had more intensive ties among the mobile, nuclear families. The data in this respect did not reveal any significant differences from the traditional, expanded families. Thus, both types of families appeared to have the same proportion of intimate relationships within the conjugal family unit.

This finding may be interpreted in many ways. It may be that differences really do exist but were not detected because of the measurements used. For example, no effort was made to collect data on parent-child relations or sibling relationships which might have revealed differences. On the other hand, one cannot also discount the possibility that there may have been some latent factors at work such as would be related to pride and family honor. Among the traditionals, this may have led to a tendency to exaggerate the number of intimate family relationships while the mobiles may have felt less need to demonstrate such family "closeness" to others. Another more likely explanation is that intimate relationships within the conjugal family unit are about the same but the traditionals also have close relations with more relatives. The mobiles may in a sense neutralize their extended kinship ties because of wider interests, other friendship ties, and the like.

Another significant finding should be explained which concerns friendship ties. It was found that the expanded families extended and received help from friends more often than did the nuclear families. This would suggest a greater reliance on mutual help patterns generally and is therefore not only related to the family. Perhaps pride related to rugged individualism and pride in the conjugal unit are factors which prevent the nuclear families from seeking help or saying that help is needed. This would stand in contrast to the traditional sub-system which, apparently, is conditioned to stress; and emphasizes a wider involvement of family and friends in solving day-to-day problems of living.

One final finding must be explained which was contrary to expectations as inferred in the descriptive typologies of the various families. It would be expected that a greater neighborhood identification would rest with the expanded families in the ethnic neighborhood setting. This was not found to be as evident in this case. While this might be related to faulty measurement instruments, it may be accounted for by the fact that the mobiles' tendency to be "community minded" wherever they reside would be detected in identification with the neighborhood, as measured. Furthermore, it may also be true that the "familism" of the traditionals would dictate against investment beyond the expanded family. The tendency of the traditionals to have larger proportions of formal associations is also contrary to the expectation that there would be greater involvement of mobiles in such organizations. One can only state that the findings are inconclusive in regard to neighborhood identifications. Nevertheless, both the nuclear and expanded families share attributes which would suggest involvement in neighborhood life while the deviants appear to be most detached and alienated.

There was, in this study, also an opportunity to examine attributes of mixed-type families which were associated with deviant boys. Descriptions of such families were based on the functions that these families appeared to take on by virtue of the fact that they were part of the deviant subsystem.

It was found that the deviants had family types representing the extreme forms of all the attributes considered. Thus, mixed families had the least financial resources, lowest aspirations, most distant relatives who were least involved in family affairs, and had a tendency to help each other least often. All this appears to indicate the relative lack of effective family relations among deviant boys. It might be interpreted that the behavioral styles, mutual supports and satisfactions that have strong family sanctions are therefore lacking; and results in the relative inability of deviants to become more recognized and accepted. Conflictual behavior might in a sense be symptomatic of a family type which is dysfunction inasmuch as the family is unable to suitably condition the behavior of its members in respect to the other two subsystems.

Group Types

The research regarding group types for our purposes was found to be scarce because it was noted that very little had been done empirically to see how group properties were influenced culturally or how they were related to social class. By and large, the hypotheses were based on the potential functions the properties appeared to take on regarding the members. Lacking a suitable typology, the effort was turned towards trying to clarify specific group properties by observation. Group size, membership patterns, group engagement, and cohesion were examined to see to what extent these group properties would differentiate the corner-boy, college-boy, and deviant-boy group types.

The literature on group size showed that the number of members in the group, by its effects on the interactive processes, would affect a variety of phenomena. By and large, smaller groups seemed to provide greater satisfactions. The frequency, duration, and intimacy of contacts among members were found to decrease as size increased. Smaller groups usually provided for greater unity in that communication and consensus were more easily attained. A group's membership pattern has also been seen as another property which distinguishes groups. Generally the closed group was more influential in that membership was more highly valued and group perspectives were more closely followed, while membership in open groups tended to be less valued and group perspectives less closely followed. The third property, engagement in the group, ranged from the totalitarian type, which involved members wholly and regulated their partication completely, to the segmented type, which involved its members in more limited ways. And finally, the cohesive quality of groups was noted as a most significant although sometimes elusive group property. It was noted that the greater the cohesion, the greater the influence on the membership, and the greater the likelihood of member satisfaction.

According to the findings, these group properties served to differentiate the group types to greater or lesser degrees. Differences in group size and engagement in the group were not found to be statistically significant although differences were found to exist. The corner-boy and college-boy groups and some of the deviant-boy groups were found to be smaller in size and as such may have reflected greater satisfactions. The greater number of larger groups among the deviants likewise suggests that there would be less satisfactions, intimacy, and unity among some deviant groups. While these slight differences in group size existed, the data concerning engagement in groups were contradictory. In the main, deviant-boy groups were found to be more totalitarian in that they were reputed to have members more often and more totally involved in group activities.

This was not consistent with the other findings regarding the relatively open membership of the deviant-boy group and the lack of cohesiveness it revealed. The deviant boys who involved themselves in larger groups may actually be unable to relate appropriately within the smaller group which is more demanding and requires greater adherence to group goals. The fact that more state that they were totally involved may actually represent wishful thinking contrary to other data. Support for this interpretation is evident in that deviant boys more often tended to be members of many groups; and it did not appear likely that they could be "totally involved" as much as was indicated. Conversely, the traditional boys' greater attention to only one or a few groups supports the contention that the corner-boy group, by its smaller size, close and cohesive nature, is in all likelihood more engaging of its members than was determined when compared to the deviant-boy groups.

The differences that were found regarding open versus closed groups and group cohesion were more conclusive in that the differences were statistically significant. Although it was found that the corner-boy groups were more often closed, and the college-boy groups were more often open a-cording to the criteria used, the deviant boy groups were not as clearly differentiated. Members of the deviant-boy groups appeared to be members of open groups but stated their preferences for closed groups. Following the same line of reasoning used above, this too may be a matter of wishful thinking inasmuch as it is not consistent with the other data regarding the deviant-boy groups. One possible interpretation is that the deviant boys belong to larger and more open groups but sense a certain dissatisfaction regarding group adjustment. According to this view, responses which indicate a desire for smaller, more closed groups would reflect the fact that their present group type was dysfunctional for them.

On the other hand, there is in this instance an added factor which should be noted although its significance could not be tested because of the extremely small number of cases observed. Among the deviant boys indicating preferences for open groups by far the greater proportion were younger in age. This conceivably would support in a very tentative and unsubstantiated way the theoretical distinctions made between the potential delinquent and delinquent groups. While all conflicting boys were combined in this study, perhaps differences in group size, open versus closed membership patterns, and the degree of engagement were in some way related to the degree to which conflicting boys were either still seeking or had already achieved a "delinquent solution." On the assumption that the younger boys were more likely to be potential delinquent, their preferences for open groups might reflect the greater functional utility of open groups for these boys, while the closed group is more functional for the full-fledged delinquents. There was, however, no attempt to differentiate boys who had in effect reached a delinquent solution. Furthermore, questions still persist inasmuch as there were apparently no other indications of age differences in the sample.

Perhaps the most dramatic differences were reflected in the cohesive properties as they were related to group types. The evidence strongly illustrated the greater cohesiveness of the corner-boy groups as measured by sociometric attraction. The college-boy groups were moderately cohesive, while the deviant-boy groups were the least cohesive.

The data may be interpreted to mean that mutual relationships and ties which the traditionals are able to establish are meaningful and binding in their groups. The corner-boy group member is more likely to have friends and members of groups which are based on intimate and mutually recognized ties. The mobiles have friends and members of groups who are not as mutually responsive in their group associations. The deviants, on the other hand, reported many friends and members of groups, but these appear to lack meaning in that seldom do these friends and group members reciprocate such recognition. The lack of unity and consensus regarding friendships and group associations was therefore readily apparent.

The close relationship between the variables (values, family types and peer group associations) viewed in the context of functional theory or analysis implies that the attributes of one variable bear some functional relation to the other two. Thus, for example, strong group solidarity as a value is reflected in the larger "solid" family group and other group preferences which require close-ties, cohesion, etc. One attribute may have as a counterpart some attribute or set of attributes in the other variable which are consistent with each other. In this sense, one variable may be viewed as it "conditions" the other two.[4]

But, it may also be that one variable attribute or set of attributes may be quite different in that one serves some purpose or function relative to the other for which the other is not equipped. It may be true, for example, that the greater family involvement of the traditionals does not permit the existing boy as part of a larger family network, to be the relatively simple center of affection and security that is possible in the close-knit nuclear family. The greater adherence to the single, close-knit friendship group might in a sense make up such a deficiency and thus be functionally useful.[5]

There is also, of course, the additional circumstance where one variable may be both functional and dysfunctional when examined in light of different contexts. An example of this is seen where the openness of the potential delinquent group may be functional for the individual seeking solutions to problems of adjustment by helping him to meet others and eventually resolve his mixed status. The open group is, however, dysfunctional as it does not easily permit its members to develop greater intimacy and mutual support which may be psychologically securing. Another example would be the mixed family type which may be functional since it permits greater mobility allowing its members to move independently; but, which would be viewed to be dysfunctional in Little Italy where it is not able to support and condition its members to deal effectively with the prevalent neighborhood style of life which requires effective family support.

One is consequently caught up with the dilemma of determining whether or not an attribute in one or another variable can be viewed to be functional or dysfunctional. This continues to demonstrate a need for a clearer conception of criteria for determining the functional usefulness of one or another variable, attribute, type, or property with an equally clear designation of the frame of reference upon which any relationship is to be evaluated.

Implications Regarding the Role of the Settlement

Although it has been generally accepted that settlement houses are
meant to serve neighborhoods, there has been much confusion regarding
the make-up of their clientele. Whyte,[6] Cohen,[7] and Gans,[8] for example,
have leveled criticism which in the main holds that the settlement car-
ries middle-class values and thereby fails to reach into the lives of
the working-class boys in any relevant way. Such a middle-class value
orientation furthermore tends to favor the upward mobile or potentially
mobile youngsters.

This kind of study can give some guide lines which will help agencies to be more explicit and precise in analyzing the composition of
membership or service populations. The study of a neighborhood in terms
of subsystem differentiation furthermore makes it more likely that program development will take into account the differential interactions
that each of the subsystems maintains. For example, it has been shown
how the upward mobile adhere to the structured, role-oriented, goal-
formulated activities; while the traditional subsystem prefers the spontaneous, person-to-person, non-directed activities. By careful attention to these types of differential involvement, the settlement can determine more systematically the nature of its membership and can dis-
cover ways in which one or another segment of the neighborhood is likely to be affected by policy or program changes.

To be sure, social workers hold to certain values which are com-
municated to those with whom they work. The nature of such value orientations need, of course, to be understood in order to recognize and
fully appreciate how values enter into the treatment process. But to
say that social workers carry middle-class values as persons does not
necessarily mean that the values of the profession are confined to the
enhancement of middle-class values. To be sure, social work values or
ideological commitments can and should apply throughout the continuum
of class orientations. It should be clear that within the stable working class order itself, there are styles of life which contain "strengths"
which, when furthered, are entirely consistent with social work goals.
For example, close family ties, mutual assistance and help patterns,
person-to-person orientations, close cohesive groups, etc. which were
found to be indigenous to working-class boys may be desirable attributes
which could functionally be helpful for growing personalities.

Group work emphasizes the importance of effective social relationships appropriate for each stage of social development to encourage the
fullest realization of the potential personality of each individual.
There is nothing inherent in this kind of statement that would confine
its applicability to the stable working-class, middle or upward mobile
class, or any other class of people. Rather, it would appear to be a
matter of appropriately relating social work goals to the particular
social system or relevant subsystem. This can only be done after a
thorough analysis of the subsystems and their functional interrelationships has been accomplished.

To the extent that agencies continue to use one set of criteria
for evaluating all the clients alike without regard to their subsystem
identifications they will overlook opportunities to develop differential programs and will run the risk of being insensitive and unrespon-
sive to social need. For example, aiding in the push for upward mobility may actually create more problems -- when done without an under-

standing of the circumstances. Blau,[9] in this connection has advanced the view that certain kinds of mobility create special dilemmas for interpersonal relations. Within the stable working-class style of life there may be many overlooked strengths and potentials for its members which may serve as goals for settlements for certain clients. Supporting solely a middle class or upwards mobile value structure would be inappropriate.

This is the conclusion that Miller and Riesman come to in their analysis of the stable working class. Noting a tendency on the part of educational and other institutions to deal with working-class youth to "middle-class size" them, they state, "possibly there is a better chance of emphasizing working-class values; for example, cooperation -- as happens in group therapy -- rather than vocational success in middle class terms."[10]

The suggestion that certain working-class values serve as models for intervention has many implications in practice. The goals for the potential delinquent youth or the corner-boy are therefore not set in terms of the upward mobile population necessarily. Yet, many program activities are offered as though this were the case. Consider the efforts on the part of workers to help such groups take on appropriate "formal roles," "go through agency channels," etc. Many such efforts are doomed to failure. The role orientation of the middle class then is simply not suitable. The gap is too great. The significance or relevancy to deviant-boy groups and corner-boy groups is at best marginal. An emphasis on the casual, personal, and free autonomous group participation which is consistent with the traditional system may be much more to the point.

The stable working-class orientation may be a necessary prerequisite for later movement which should be considered in any attempt to help the deviant-boy take on the college-boy responses. Miller and Riessman state the following in this respect:

> It is not intrinsic in the stable pattern that a middle class orientation emerge but the stable stage would seem to be a necessary step in most cases for the development of a middle class orientation.[11]

While this may hold true as a general guide in differentially working with the diverse subsystem members, one must recognize also that there are some dangers in using one group as a kind of model for another. Does this mean, for example, that the deviant-boy group would be encouraged to take on the whole corner-boy adaptation regarding for example, obvious hostility to outsiders, non-utilization of personal and social resources and opportunities, etc.? Certainly not. It merely indicates that there are certain potentialities within the stable working class subculture which should be carefully explored as to their advantages and fruitfulness in working with deviant boys.

One other point remains to be made concerning strategies for intervention with respect to the subsystems. Among suggested functions for settlements, Gans suggests that they should seek to more intensively serve people aspiring to middle-class ways, and to provide less intensive services to the remaining larger proportion of the neighborhood population. Speaking of these two functions, he states:

This second function should be strictly demarcated from
the first one (perhaps even through separate buildings),
so that the two types of clients -- who are quite different in their characteristics and needs -- do not get
in each other's way, or more important, do not stay away
from the settlement house because each believes that the
house is only interested in the other.[12]

Aside from the fact that such a statement obviously misunderstands
the settlement house movement and commitment to help people accept each
other and their differences, in terms of our discussion this approach
has very little theoretical support. Although the functional relationships between the three subsystems were not investigated, the patterns
which were discovered supported the contention that patterned interactions of one subsystem will be influenced by and in turn influence
those of the other -- the most dramatic example theoretically being the
emergence of the delinquent subculture as a response to the middle-
class value system. If this is the case one can hardly hope to amelio-
rate the situation by isolating one from another through separate pro-
gramming, for to do so would be to work with symptoms and neglect the
causes. As any settlement house worker knows, it is difficult to work
with such groups in combination. But to follow a course of action that
in essence merely provides programs for non-mobiles who simply want to
come to the settlement to use facilities they cannot obtain or afford
elsewhere, is to carve out a fairly easy piece of the problem. This
study has demonstrated that each subsystem has attributes which are related to its own particular orientation. It remains for the practition-
er to fashion the appropriate strategies for all in a manner which
recognizes the interrelationships between them.

The findings clearly indicate that a group worker's knowledge of
the social cultural aspects of the neighborhood cannot be confined to
the sector where the neighborhood and the agency come together. Indeed, every individual has to be seen as he fits into the social scheme
of things. This would imply, therefore, that in the diagnosis of clients (relative to social facts) an effort will be made to place him not
only in terms of any group of which he happens to be a member but relative to a social network of relations which distinguishes large numbers
of individuals, families, and groups as they are susceptible to social
influences. We turn next to a consideration of the implications this
has for group work practice.

Implications for Group Practice

This study, in part, grew from the recognition that while the group
worker very often was able to be specific about internal group processes
affecting group behavior, he lacked the conceptual tools to be as specific in dealing with what was more generally regarded as the external
"social influences". In terms of practice, this often gives the worker
the feeling that no matter what is attempted or accomplished within the
group, the chances of bringing about significant change continues to be
strongly influenced by external social forces beyond the reach of the
worker. Although generalized influences doubtless will continue to be
operative and difficult to detect, this study suggests a way to be more
specific about such influences.

Thus, in the rendering of service, the potential for giving help to individuals in and through the use of the group in its more internal aspects is broadened to include specific criteria regarding the group's place in the total social configuration consisting of individuals, families, and groups in interaction. Attention will accordingly be focused on the entire network of systemic linkages and boundary maintenance processes which differentially affect the group depending upon the part it plays in this overall pattern. The group's position will shed light on which intervention strategies beyond the group should be considered in determining a focus for service.

While internal and external distinctions continue to be useful analytically, this study highlights the intimate relationship which exists between the two levels of conceptualization. Some of the implications this has for the practice of group work will be considered from this vantage point.

In group work a thorough understanding and knowledge of group processes is a necessary prerequisite for sound practice. Of particular importance are such processes as are related to group formation with the emergence of group goals, membership, and structural differentiation; interpersonal relations; communication and deliberation, the group's culture; and emotional climate. The worker, in essence is responsible for knowing how and when to intervene with respect to these processes to bring about the desired goals. Sometimes he helps set the stage by encouraging the development of one or another process such as when he seeks to affect the group's formal or informal structure, to modify its decision-making procedures, or to affect its social climate. This is done, of course, to facilitate clearly specified goals regarding the social functioning of the members. At other times, his knowledge of these processes permits him to use his relationships with the group and its members to deal constructively with the influences of the group. In any event, the group processes intimately affect individual members and enter into every practice problem.

The findings suggest that the group worker's concepts of these group processes can be extended to include simultaneously related processes at work in other social systems such as, for example, the family. Consequently, the corner-boy group may characteristically display attributes which may be reflective of the way the expanded family functions. Attempts to modify the close-knit, cohesive properties of these groups may therefore be greatly facilitated by corresponding attention to the roles boys play as members of expanded families. Until such boys are able to adopt individual responsibilities and become more independent from the family, it may be most difficult to modify the solidarity of the corner-boy group or help the group's cohesiveness take on different meanings for its members. To take another example, the absence of significant family ties among deviants corresponds with the greater tendency of deviant-boy groups to avoid close and mutually obligatory relationships. Efforts to develop cohesion within certain of the deviant-boy groups may prove to be in conflict with the major function the group provides for its members, as a mechanism for solving problems of adjustment. Such groups provide for less intensive relations in a "safe" kind of way.

This broader perspective on group processes also serves to guide the worker's diagnostic thinking in directions which may be innovative in practice. For example, very little is known about how extended relatives may be encouraged to take on meaningful roles in relation to boys' groups. In the case of the corner-boy group, the influence of uncles, brothers-in-law, cousins, godfathers, etc. can have a significant impact. They may be encouraged to become useful allies in furthering social work objectives.

Another implication for group work practice stems from the fact that groups may also be found to bear significant relationships to each other. Furthermore, groups relate across subsystems as well as within subsystems and may therefore reflect differential group types and individual value orientations in combination. Thus, the deviant-boy group in the deviant subsystem may be unattracted to the college-boy group in the traditional subsystem. It may be that the deviant-boy group may take on instrumental functions in bidding for recognition from the corner-boy group which enjoys higher status and effective family backing. The nature of the resulting relationships which are developed are affected accordingly and will have some consequences on the group processes which evolve.

The point is that group workers must take into account the way groups are or are not significantly linked to each other. This could lead to the practice of taking on or assigning groups for service not as separate groups as is often done, but as part of a set of groups taking into account characteristic linkages or boundary maintenance patterns. Groups will thereby be considered in units or clusters of two or more groups which will make it possible for the agency to bring the resources of the agency to bear directly on the unit as influences are specified relative to any single group.[13] Such a unit can be determined in terms of similar or dissimilar identification, or it may include groups from different age levels. Whatever the unit, the worker will be in a position to do something about the characteristic linkages that occur and affect behavior. This concept, of course, does not necessarily mean that the unit of groups must have the same common worker although the advantages of using one worker appear to be evident. Such a person is in a position to more systematically help the various groups internally while at the same time he can consistently deal specifically with the linkages which occur externally.

Although the concept of the neighborhood has been greatly refined here in terms of interacting social systems, generally the findings were not entirely new or different. Social workers, for example, have known for some time that values were related to family living and that any effort to change individual values might require a similar effort to work with the family as well. Also, in group work it is axiomatic that changing the value system of the group will have some effect on the way the individual member must deal with his own values relative to the group.

The evidence clearly illustrates the linkages between the variables but leaves many questions unanswered about where the most strategic and parsimonious point of intervention should be. While it may appear that change can be precipitated in one variable by intervening in another, our knowledge in this regard remains vague. Would structural changes in the group bring about value changes in the individual? Can certain changes in group properties be brought about that in turn affect group functions? It is obvious that much more needs to be known before answers to such questions can be given. Furthermore, it does not necessarily follow that intervention in one variable will bring about the desired results in another for no cause and effect relationships have been proved. Wherever intervention is applied, there remains the question of how to reinforce and support the desired outcomes by appropriately dealing with the other social variables. Moreover, since it is obvious that the interrelationships or linkages between the variables are extensively interwoven, the social configuration may appear to have a greater tendency to obstruct change than is generally realized.

This study has clearly shown in a most specific manner the nature of certain of the social variable attributes which are operative in regard to individual value orientations, family patterns, and group associations. These appear to be important elements in the analysis of social influences. This study did not examine causal relationships which may help determine points of intervention. But, it does show that whatever the treatment of choice, attempts to affect one variable cannot proceed effectively without corresponding attention to the relationships, influences, and counter-influences of the other two variables.

FOOTNOTES--CHAPTER IV

[1]Although the study was stimulated by a desire to know more about how the various subsystems were functionally related, by necessity one first had to establish that such subsystems existed. This study was designed to accomplish this. A more exacting knowledge of the functional relationships of subsystems remains for future programmatic research.

[2]For a most current study reporting this finding see Janus F. Short, Jr. and Fred L. Strodtbeck, Group Process and Gang Delinquency (Chicago, Illinois: University of Chicago Press, 1965) pp. 59-76. This finding fits well with the concept of the lower-class value stretch as developed by Hyman Rodman, "The Lower Class Value Stretch" XLII Social Forces (December, 1963) 205-15. In this view the lower class person, without abandoning the general values of society, develops an alternate set as well and thus has a wider range of values.

[3]It may be recalled that "smartness" constitutes one of the focal concerns of lower-class boys as viewed by Walter B. Miller, "Lower Class Culture as a Generating Milieu of Gang Delinquency," Journal of Social Issues XIV (1958), 5-19.

[4]An example of this kind of relationship appears to exist between certain instrumental and expressive functions evident in the family which tend to be similarly reflected in groups. See Talcott Parsons and Robert E. Bales, Family: Socialization and Interaction (Glencoe, Illinois: The Free Press, 1955), pp. 299-306.

[5]A good example of this kind of functional relationship is found in S. N. Eisenstadt, From Generation to Generation: Age Groups and Social Structure (Illinois: The Free Press, 1956) which in essence states that the peer group with its universalistic qualities is functionally better able to aid the individual move into society than the family which is overly particularistic for such a task.

[6]William F. Whyte, Street Corner Society: The Social Structure of an Italian Slum (2nd ed. re.; Chicago: University of Chicago Press, 1955), p. 104.

[7]Albert Cohen, Delinquent Boys: The Culture of the Gang (Glencoe, Illinois: The Free Press, 1955), p. 116.

[8]Herbert Gans. The Urban Villagers: Group and Class in the Life of Italian-Americans (Glencoe, Illinois: The Free Press of Glencoe), pp. 148-162.

[9]Peter Blau, "Social Mobility and Interpersonal Relations," American Sociological Review, XXI (June, 1956), 290-295. See also, Melvin Tumin, "Some Unapplauded Consequences of Social Mobility in a Mass Society," Social Forces, XXXVI (October, 1957), 32-37.

[10]S. M. Miller and Frank Riessman, "The Working Class Sub-Culture: A New View," Social Problems IX (Summer, 1961), p. 96.

[11]Ibid.

[12]Herbert Gans, "Redefining the Settlement's Function for the War on Poverty," Social Work, IX (October, 1964) p. 12.

[13]It must also be recognized that just as there are units of groups there can be units of families as well. Increasingly, there is interest in working with the family as a group. It may be equally important to view the family as a part of a unit of families for the findings do suggest that there are similarities based on subsystem attributes.

APPENDIX A
(Letter Introducing Study to Parents)

ALTA SOCIAL SETTLEMENT
12510 Mayfield Road . Cleveland 6, Ohio

Dear Mr. and Mrs. _____,

    For some time now Alta House has been trying out new ways of work-
ing with boys in clubs at the Settlement House. In order to have the
best kind of program possible it is important to know more about the
neighborhood and the families from which the boys come.

    I have been engaged in a study of the neighborhood boys between
the ages of 12 and 18. Through my interviews with these boys, which
included your son, I have a group of parents whom we would like to
talk with to get information, help and advice.

    An interviewer from Alta House will call on both of you in the
next few days. I sincerely hope that you will be kind enough to give
about forty minutes of your time to help us in this important study.

    If you have any questions, please don't hesitate to call me at
Alta House at any time.

                          Sincerely yours,

                          Albert S. Alissi
                          Director

WHAT DO YOU THINK QUESTIONNAIRE

Name: Address:

Birthdate: School: Grade:

Below you will find fourteen statements which everyone thinks different about. Please read each statement and if you strongly agree circle the large YES. If you agree but not as strongly, circle the smaller yes. If you don't agree circle the small no. If you strongly disagree circle the big NO. Only circle one answer for each statement.

THIS IS NOT A TEST. THERE ARE NO RIGHT OR WRONG ANSWERS.

---

1. It's best to live for today and not worry about tomorrow.

    YES   yes   no   NO

2. If I were an usher at a movie, I would let my friends in free.

    YES   yes   no   NO

3. Every guy should be responsible for himself and not expect the guys in his clique to cover for each other.

    YES   yes   no   NO

4. I don't stay interested in the things I do but I soon get bored and look for something else to do.

    YES   yes   no   NO

5. If I had nothing to do I would just hang around.

    YES   yes   no   NO

6. I like to sit down, talk and plan things to do with my free time.

    YES   yes   no   NO

7. Reading books and studying is mostly a waste of time because you really learn from experience.

    YES   yes   no   NO

8. No matter what happened, I would always stick with my own clique.

    YES   yes   no   NO

9. If I were elected president of an organization, I would treat everyone according to the rules--even my friends.

    YES   yes   no   NO

10. The most important thing in life is to be able to do things well.

    YES   yes   no   NO

11. People should give up things and sacrifice to be ready for the future.

    YES   yes   no   NO

12. I don't waste time planning what to do because I can always find something at the last minute.

    YES   yes   no   NO

13. I'm already doing things now for what I want way in the future.

    YES   yes   no   NO

14. People with a lot of education give the best advice about life.

    YES   yes   no   NO

APPENDIX C

Instructions   "Boys in Little Italy"

<u>JUDGES VALUE RATINGS</u>

We are interested in discovering ways of helping our youth to find new and constructive ways of behaving. You will be given a card index of all the boys between the ages of twelve and eighteen who live in this neighborhood. Would you please rate all of those boys who are known to you according to the three different categories as described? Judges ratings will be held in the strictest of confidence.

Col. 1.   Each card contains identifying data such as name, nickname, age, address, etc. for each boy. The case number after the name corresponds with the case number in Col. 1 of the Boys Value Ratings which you are asked to fill out.

Col. 2.   Indicate whether or not you know the boy. Simply check (✓) <u>yes</u> or <u>no</u>. A yes answer means you know him well enough to rate him according to the categories described below in Col. 3, 4, and 5. If you answer no make <u>no</u> other checks and move on to the next card.

Col. 3.   <u>Achieving</u>. Put a check (✓) in this column if the boy displays a majority of the following characteristics:
           Appears to want to get ahead in life.
           Does not waste his time but uses it constructively.
           Is responsible for his own individual actions.
           Assumes responsibility as a member of organized groups.
           Thinks and plans for the future.
           Is out to accomplish, achieve success, and perform well.
           Appreciates and values an education.

Col. 4.   <u>Being</u>. Put a check (✓) in this column if the boy displays a majority of the following characteristics:
           Does not appear to want to get ahead in life but rather just tries to get by.
           Spends much of his free time "hanging around."
           Is a real part of the clique he hangs with and his actions always reflect the group's influence.
           While he is somewhat apathetic, he has many short-range interests that he pursues only for a while.
           He does not think much about nor does he plan for the future.
           Does not appear motivated to accomplish and achieve but rather to enjoy things the way they are.
           Does not appreciate nor value education but is more "practical" minded.

Col. 5.   <u>Conflicting</u>. Put a check (✓) in this column if the boy displays a majority of the following characteristics:
           Appears to be in trouble in the neighborhood quite often.
           Stands out as being different from many of the other boys.

100

Is known as a trouble-maker and is often in conflict.
Many consider him to be a "problem" because he does not
   get along with his peers or with adults with authority.
Has status of an "outsider".
While he may not be in trouble he is viewed as a "character" who is likely to get into trouble.

Be sure to check only one of the three columns--the one which most
suitably fits the boys in question. In Col. 6 put any additional comments you would like to make.

SAMPLE

Col. 1. Case Number Identification	2. Yes	No	3. Achieving	4. Being	5. Con-flicting	6. Com-ments
1.						
2.						
3.						
4.						

APPENDIX D

BOYS IN LITTLE ITALY

PARENTS INTERVIEW SCHEDULE

1, 2, 3. Name: 4. Sex: 1) Fa_____   2) Mo_____

Address:

5. Marital Status: (1) Living with spouse ___   (2) Separated ___
                      (3) Divorced ___   (4) Spouse deceased ___
                      (5) If not first marriage, explain _____

6. Age: (1) 35 yrs. and under ___   (2) 36 to 40 yrs. ___   (3) 41 to 45
        (4) 46 to 50 yrs. ___   (5) 51 yrs. and over ___ yrs.

7. Place of birth: _____ (1) In neighborhood? ___
                 City   State
    Father: _____   (2) In neighborhood? ___
    Mother: _____   (3) In neighborhood? ___

8. Childhood spent in this neighborhood: (1) Yes ___   (2) No ___

9. Nationality: (1) Italian ___   (2) Other _____
                                   (specify)

10. Religion: (1) Catholic ___   (2) Protestant ___   (3) Jewish ___
            (4) Other (specify) _____

11. Education: (last year completed)
            (1) No schooling ___   (2) 1st through 8th grade ___
            (3) 9th, 10th, or 11th ___   (4) High School 12th ___
            (5) Incomplete College ___ (6) Completed College ___
            (7) Post graduate ___ (specify) ___

12. Special Training:

13. Occupation held up to present time: (specify in chronological order)

14. Length of family's residence in this neighborhood:
           (1) less than one yr. ___   (2) one to three years ___
           (3) three to five years ___ (4) five to ten years ___
           (5) ten to twenty years ___ (6) twenty years and over ___

15. Kind of residence: (1) rent ___   (2) own ___   (3) living with
                                            relatives ___

16. Type of dwelling: (1) single ___   (2) double ___   (3) three or
                                             more ___

17. Plans for future residence:
    (1) remain in same house ____
    (2) remain in same neighborhood but different house ____
    (3) move elsewhere ____ Specify where _____
        when _____ why _____

18. Others in household in addition to parents and children: _____

19, 20. Ages of children:
    (1) under 6 yrs. ____ males ____ females
    (2) 6 to 11 yrs. ____ males ____ females
    (3) 12 to 18 yrs. ____ males ____ females
    (4) 19 and over ____ males ____ females

21,22. Number in household attending schools:
    (1) none ____   (6) sr. high (public) ____
    (2) elementary (public) ____   (7) sr. high (parochial) ____
    (3) elementary (parochial) ____ (8) College _____
    (4) jr. high (public) ____   (specify)
    (5) jr. high (parochial) ____ (9) Others _____ _____
                                        (specify)

23. Should this neighborhood have a high school here?
    (1) yes ____   (2) no ____   Explain why _____

24. Educational desires for children:
         Males   Females
    Age ____ Plan _____   Age ____ Plan _____
    ____   _____   ____   _____
    ____   _____   ____   _____

25. Occupational desires for children:
         Males   Females
    Age ____ Plan _____   Age ____ Plan _____
    ____   _____   ____   _____
    ____   _____   ____   _____

26. Educational achievements of Relatives: (last grade completed)
    Maternal grandfather _____
    Paternal grandfather _____
    Father _____

27. Occupations of Relatives: (major occupation)
    Maternal grandfather _____
    Paternal grandfather _____
    Father _____

28. Present Family Income Bracket: (hand respondant Income Bracket Card)
    (1) under $3000 ____
    (2) $3000 - $6000 ____
    (3) $6000 - $9000 ____
    (4) Over $9000 ____

29. Estimated social class position:
    (1) upper ____   (2) middle ____   (3) working ____   (4) lower
                                                              ____

30. Kin Relationships: (Family of Orientation)*

Relative	RELATIONSHIP				RESIDENCE		
	Intimate	Effective	Non-Effective	Unfamiliar	Neighborhood	Clev.	Out of Cle.
	1	2	3	4			
(Grandparents)							
(Parents)							
(Uncles, Aunts, Cousins)							
(Brothers, Spouse children)							
(Sisters, Spouse, children)							

*Original schedule included additional chart for Family of Procreation.

31. Relationships with children and grandchildren out of household.

RELATIONSHIP				RESIDENCE		
Intimate 1	Effective 2	Non-Effective 3	Unfamiliar 4	Neighborhood	Clev.	Out of Clev.

32. Family Gatherings (List occasions)

	(1) Part of the Family	(2) Entire Family	(3) Family and Intimate Relatives Only	(4) All Available Relatives
(1) New Year's				
(2) Easter				
(3) Fourth of July				
(4) Feast of Assumption - Aug. 15				
(5) Thanksgiving				
(6) Christmas				
(7) Birthdays				
(8) Anniversaries				
(9) Christening and Communions				
(10) Weddings				
(11) Funerals				
(12) Others				

33. a. Who makes decisions for family when troubles occur:
   1. Husband ___
   2. Wife ___
   3. Both ___
   4. Other (specify) ___

33. b. Have you ever been called upon to make decisions for relatives:
   5. Often ___
   6. Sometimes ___
   7. Never ___

34. a. Main source of help in times of trouble:
    1. Family ___
    2. Relatives ___
    3. Friends ___
    4. Others (specify) ___

34. b. Do you often give help to relatives:
    5. Often ___
    6. Sometimes ___
    7. Never ___
    Do you give help to friends:
    8. Often ___   9. Sometimes ___
    10. Never ___

35. a. Help with finances.
    1. Relatives ___
    2. Friends ___
    3. Banks ___
    4. Others (specify) ___

35. b. Do you help relatives financially:
    5. Often ___   6. Sometimes ___
    7. Never ___
    Do you help friends financially: 8. Often ___
    9. Sometimes ___
    10. Never ___

36. a. Help with care of children:
    1. Relatives ___
    2. Friends ___
    3. Babysitters ___
    4. Others (specify) ___

36. b. Do you help relatives with their children:
    5. Often ___   6. Sometimes ___
    7. Never ___
    Do you help friends:
    8. Often ___   9. Sometimes ___
    10. Never ___

37. a. Help with personal problems:
    1. Family ___
    2. Relatives ___
    3. Friends ___
    4. Professionals ___

37. b. Do you help relatives with their personal problems:
    5. Often ___
    6. Sometimes ___
    7. Never ___
    Do you help friends with their personal problems:
    8. Often ___
    9. Sometimes ___
    10. Never ___

38. When did you last visit a relative?

    1. Today _____
    2. Within last week _____
    3. Within last month _____
    4. Last 3 months _____
    5. Last year _____
    6. Over a year _____

39. When did a relative last visit you?

    _____
    _____
    _____
    _____
    _____
    _____

INFORMAL NEIGHBORHOOD AND COMMUNITY CONTACTS

40. Which of the following statements is nearest your opinion of the people in this neighborhood?
    1. They are hard to get to know ___ or

        2. They are easy to get to know ___.
        3. They are hard to get along with ___ or
        4. They are easy to get along with.

41. Do you feel you are a part of this neighborhood?
        1. Like most of the neighborhood ___
        2. Like a certain segment ___ why _____
        3. Different from most people or any segment ___ why _____

42. Name persons whom you feel are "key" people in the neighborhood:
        1. _____   why _____
        2. _____   why _____
        3. _____   why _____

43. Relationship with key persons: 1.   2.   3.   4.   5.
        Not personally acquainted   _____
        Personally acquainted   _____
        Spend some time together   _____
        Discuss general topics together   _____
        Discuss personal topics   _____

44. Name your closest friends: How long known to you   Neighborhood
                                                         Residence

        1. _____   _____   _____
        2. _____   _____   _____
        3. _____   _____   _____

45. FORMAL NEIGHBORHOOD AND COMMUNITY CONTACTS:

        Membership in clubs and organizations:

	Attendance			Offices	Membership	Financial
	Always	Often	Seldom	Held	in Committees	Contribution
Church Groups						
School Groups (PTA)						
(PTU)						
Social Lodges						
Unions						
Political Groups						
Athletic Groups						
Neighborhood Council						

46. Do you have a library card? 1. yes ___   2. no ___
    If yes, do you take out books to read? 3. always ___ 4. often ___
                                           5. sometimes ___ 6. never __

47. Do you read daily newspapers? 1. always___   2. often ___
                                  3. sometimes ___   4. never ___

48. People in the neighborhood differ with regard to how they like
    living here. Below are a list of factors some people like and
    some people dislike. Indicate if you agree with the statement,
    and if so, whether you consider this to be attractive or unattrac-
    tive.

	Yes	Attractive	Unattractive
It is cheaper to live here.	1. ____	1. ____	1. ____
Everyone knows everyone else.	2. ____	2. ____	2. ____
It's like one big "happy family."	3. ____	3. ____	3. ____
It is secure and safe.	4. ____	4. ____	4. ____
It has a reputation for being tough.	5. ____	5. ____	5. ____
It has an Italian flavor.	6. ____	6. ____	6. ____
It remains independent and isolated.	7. ____	7. ____	7. ____
It's informal and not snobbish.	8. ____	8. ____	8. ____

49. Do your sons belong to any Alta House Clubs? (1) Yes____ (2) No ____

50. What suggestions would you have to make about the kinds of clubs that Alta House should have?

51. Do you have any suggestions about new or different activities that Alta House should offer?

INTERVIEWER'S COMMENTS:

_____   _____
Interviewer   Date

107

DESCRIBE YOUR GROUP QUESTIONNAIRE
Boys in Little Italy

NAME: Age: Date:

I.   (1)   Please list all of the boys who are members of the group
            or crowd you go with.

      (2)   Are there any other boys who are in the group sometimes?
            Yes___ No___   If yes, approximately how many? ___

      (3)   Are any of the members of your group new to the group?
            (i.e. joined in the last 6 months) Yes___ No___
            If yes, how many? ___

      (4)   Do you have any friends who are not in the group?
            Yes___ No___   If yes, how many? ___

      (5)   List the names of three of your closest friends
            1.
            2.
            3.

II.   Below are a list of statements about you and your group. If you
      definitely agree circle the large YES. If you agree moderately
      circle the small yes. If you disagree circle the small no. If
      you definitely disagree circle the large NO. Be sure to circle
      only one answer.

      1.   My group is made of mostly close friends. YES yes no NO
      2.   We all want the same things.   YES yes no NO
      3.   The group ranks among the best.   YES yes no NO
      4.   We all share and give up things to belong. YES yes no NO
      5.   We stick with each other rather than with
            other guys.   YES yes no NO
      6.   It's easy to become a member of my group. YES yes no NO
      7.   The group members usually feel the same
            way about hings.   YES yes no NO
      8.   It's easy to tell who's a member of my
            group.   YES yes no NO
      9.   Other groups influence my group quite a
            bit.   YES yes no NO
      10.   I'd like to stay with this group.   YES yes no NO
      11.   The group is one of the best ways to
            protect yourself from outside threats.   YES yes no NO

III. Please mark a check (✓) in the right space to show how much
      time you spend with the group in each activity. Mark only one.
      Then mark a check (✓) to show whether part of the group or

most all of the group participates in the activity.

ACTIVITIES	Always	Often	Some-times	Seldom	Never	Part of Group	Most all of Group
School (not in classroom)							
Settlement House							
Sports (Playing)							
Sports (Watching)							
Movies							
Television							
Hanging Around							
Driving Around							
Parties							
Holidays & Special Events							
Others _____							

IV. MAKE YOUR CHOICE:
(1) You are standing on the corner with your club. A friend comes over and reports that he was bounced by some guys on the other side of the tracks. The group decides to take off after the boys. Just as you are about to leave your brother calls you and says you better get home--there's trouble at home.

WHAT DO YOU DO?
Go home _____   or   Go with the group and then go
                                                 home _____

(2) Your group received grandstand tickets to the Browns football game and you are all planning to go as a group. A friend of yours who is not in the group has two special box seat tickets, one for you and one for him.

WHAT DO YOU DO?
Go with the group _____   or   Go with your friend _____

(3) You have a chance to work part-time and earn some extra money. But this means that you won't have <u>any</u> <u>time</u> to be with your group.

109

WHAT DO YOU DO?
Look for another job? _____ or   Take this job _____

(4) Your group is forming a basketball team to play in a league. Although you have enough boys there are other better players who want to join your team.

WHAT DO YOU DO?
Use these other players_____ or Keep it within the club _____

(5) Some of the older guys are going for a ride and you get a chance to go. On the way up the hill you see your group and call out to you to go with them. The older fellas stop for a light and ask you if you want to get out.

WHAT DO YOU DO?
Go for the ride _____   or   Get out and go with your
                                                      group _____

V.   You be the Expert and give us advice on what is the IDEAL GROUP. Put a check (   ) in the appropriate place to finish the sentence.

(1)   The ideal club should have the following number of members:
      a. _____ up to six members
      b. _____ seven to eleven members
      c. _____ twelve to sixteen members
      d. _____ over sixteen members

(2)   It should be
      a. _____ open to anyone who wants to belong
      b. _____ closed to most outsiders.

(3)   It should be organized
      a. _____ to operate on a short-time basis
      b. _____ to run for many years.

(4)   Clubs should
      a. _____ allow its members to come and go depending on how
                    they feel
      b. _____ expect its members to be on hand to attend its
                    affairs.

(5)   Clubs should be organized in such a way that the members
      a. _____ could still have friendship cliques in the group
      b. _____ not have small cliques in the group.

(6)   Boys should be members
      a. _____ of many different groups at the same time.
      b. _____ of only a few groups at the same time.
      c. _____ of only one group.

(7)   The ideal club has
      a. _____ only friends in it.
      b. _____ others beside friends in it.

(8)   Clubs should have meetings
      a. _____ only on regularly planned basis
      b. _____ whenever the members are around.

(9) The ideal club should
     a. _____have some purpose or goal for being.
     b. _____not need to have any particular reason for being.

BIBLIOGRAPHY

Alissi, Albert S. "Social Influences on Group Values," Social Work, X, No. 1 (January, 1965) 14-22.

Argyle, Michael. The Scientific Study of Social Behavior. London: Methuen and Co., Ltd. 1957.

Back, Kurt W. "Communication in Experimentally Created Hierarchies," in Leon Festinger, Kurt Back, Stanley Schachter, Harold H. Kelly, and John W. Thibaut. Theory and Experiment in Social Communication. Ann Arbor: Institute for Social Research, University of Michigan, 1950.

Banfield, Edward. The Moral Basis of a Backward Society. Glencoe, Illinois: The Free Press, 1958.

Barron, Milton L. "Juvenile Delinquency and American Values," American Sociological Review, XVI (April, 1951), 208-14.

Bell, Norman W., and Vogel, Ezra F. (eds.). A Modern Introduction to the Family. Glencoe, Illinois: The Free Press of Glencoe, 1960.

Bendix, Reinhard and Lipset, Seymour Martin (eds.). Class, Status, and Power: A Reader in Social Stratification. Glencoe, Illinois: The Free Press of Glencoe, 1963.

Blau, Peter. "Social Mobility and Interpersonal Relations," American Sociological Review, XXI (June, 1956) 290-95.

Bohlke, Robert H. "Social Mobility, Stratification Inconsistency and Middle Class Delinquency," Social Problems, VIII (Spring, 1961) 351-63.

Bordua, David J. "Delinquent Subcultures: Sociological Interpretations of Gang Delinquency," The Annals of The American Academy of Political and Social Science, CCCXXXVIII (November, 1961), 119-36.

Borgatta, Edgar F., and Cottrell, Jr., Leonard S. "On the Classification of Groups," Sociometry, XVIII, No. 4. (December, 1955), 409-22.

Bott, Elizabeth. Family and Social Network. London: Tavistock Publications, Ltd., 1964.

Boyde, Richard P. "The Effect of the High School on Students' Aspirations," American Journal of Sociology, LXXI (May, 1966), 628-39.

Campisi, Paul J. "The Italian Family in the United States," in Herman D. Stein, and Richard A. Cloward (eds.). Social Perspectives on Behavior. Glencoe, Illinois: The Free Press, 1958.

Cartwright, Dorwin, and Zander, Alvin (eds.). Group Dynamics: Research and Theory. 2d ed. revised. Evanston, Illinois: Row. Peterson and Co., 1960.

Child, Irvin L. Italian or American? The Second Generation in Conflict. New Haven: Yale University Press, 1943.

Clark, John P., and Wenninger, Eugene P. "Goal Orientations and Illegal Behavior Among Juveniles," Social Forces, XLII (October, 1963), 49-59.

Cloward, Richard, and Ohlin, Lloyd. Delinquency and Opportunity: A Theory of Delinquent Gangs. Glencoe, Illinois: The Free Press, 1960.

Cohen, Albert. Delinquent Boys: The Culture of the Gang. Glencoe, Illinois: The Free Press, 1955.

Cohen, Albert K., and Hodges, Jr., Harold M. "Characteristics of the Lower-Blue-Collar-Class," Social Problems, X (Spring, 1963), 303-34.

Coser, Rose Laub (ed.). The Family: Its Structure and Functions. New York: St. Martin's Press, 1964.

Davis, Allison. "The Motivation of the Under-priviledged Worker," in William F. Whyte (ed.). Industry and Society. New York: McGraw-Hill Book Co., 1946.

Davis, Kingsley and Moore, Wilbert E. "Some Principles of Stratification: A Critical Analysis," American Sociological Review, X (April, 1945), 242-49.

Dollard, John. Caste and Class in a Southern Town. New Haven: Yale University Press, 1937.

Eisenstadt, S. N. From Generation to Generation: Age Groups and Social Structure. Glencoe, Illinois: The Free Press, 1956.

Empey, LaMar T. "Social Class and Occupational Aspiration: A Comparison of Absolute and Relative Measurement," American Sociological Review, XXI (December, 1956), 703-709.

Festinger, Leon, Schachter, Stanley, and Back, Kurt. Social Pressures in Informal Groups: A Study of Human Factors in Housing. Revised ed. Stanford, California: Stanford University Press, 1963.

Fischer, Paul H. "An Analysis of the Primary Group," Sociometry, XVI, No. 3, (August, 1953), 272-76.

Frazier, Franklin E. "The Negro Family in the United States," in Herman D. Stein, and Richard A. Cloward (eds.). Social Perspectives on Behavior. Glencoe, Illinois: The Free Press, 1958.

Gans, Herbert J. "Redefining the Settlement's Functions for the War on Poverty," Social Work, IX, No. 4, (October, 1964) 3-12.

Gans, Herbert. The Urban Villagers: Group and Class in the Life of Italian-Americans. Glencoe, Illinois: The Free Press of Glencoe, 1962.

Gerth, H. H., and Mills, C. Wright (trans. and eds.). From Max Weber: Essays in Sociology. New York: Oxford University Press, 1946.

Glazer, Nathan. American Judaism. Chicago: University of Chicago Press, 1957.

Glazer, Nathan and Moynihan, Daniel Patrick. Beyond the Melting Pot: The Negroes, Puerto Ricans, Jews, Italians, and Irish of New York City. Cambridge, Massachusetts: The M.I.T. Press and Harward University Press, 1963.

Goffman, Erving. Behavior in Public Places: Notes on the Social Organization of Gatherings. Glencoe, Illinois: The Free Press, 1963.

Goffman, Erving. The Presentation of Self in Everyday Life. Garden City, New York: Doubleday and Co., Inc., 1959.

Golembiewski, Robert T. The Small Group: An Analysis of Research Concepts and Operations. Chicago: University of Chicago Press, 1962.

Gordon, Milton M. Social Class in American Sociology. Durham, North Carolina: Duke University Press, 1958.

Gould, Rosalind. "Some Sociological Determinants of Goal Strivings," Journal of Social Psychology XIII (May, 1941), 461-73.

Gross, Neal and Martin, William E. "On Group Cohesiveness in Small Groups," American Journal of Sociology, LVII (May, 1952) 546-54.

Hagstrom, Warren O., and Selvin, Hanan C. "Two Dimensions of Cohesiveness in Small Groups," Sociometry, XXVIII (March, 1965) 30-43.

Hare, A. Paul. "Interpersonal Relations in the Small Group," in Robert E. L. Faris (ed.). Handbook of Modern Sociology. Chicago: Rand McNally and Co., 1964.

Hausknecht, Murray. The Joiners: A Sociological Description of Voluntary Association Membership in the United States. New York: The Bedminster Press, 1962.

Hemphill, John K. Group Dimensions: A Manual for Their Measurement. Columbus, Ohio: The Ohio State University, 1956.

Hodges, Harold. Social Stratification: Class in America. Cambridge, Massachusetts: Schenkman Publishing Co., Inc., 1964.

Hoggart, Richard. The Uses of Literacy: Changing Patterns in English Mass Culture. Boston: Beacon Press, 1961.

Hollingshead, August B. "Class Differences in Family Stability," in Herman D. Stein, and Richard A. Cloward (eds.). Social Perspectives on Behavior. Glencoe, Illinois: The Free Press, 1958.

Hollingshead, August. Elmtown's Youth. New York: John Wiley and Sons, Inc., 1949.

Homans, George C. The Human Group. New York: Harcourt, Brace and
    Co., 1950.

Hopkins, Terence K. The Exercise of Influence in Small Groups. Toto-
    wa, New Jersey: The Bedminster Press, 1964.

Hyman, Herbert H. "The Values Systems of Different Classes: A Social
    Psychological Contribution to the Analysis of Stratification," in
    Reinhard Bendix and Seymour Martin Lipset (eds.). Class, Status,
    and Power: A Reader in Social Stratification. Glencoe, Illinois:
    The Free Press of Glencoe, 1963.

Kahl, Joseph A. The American Class Structure. New York: Rinehart and
    Co., Inc., 1957.

Kluckhohn, Florence. "Some Reflections on the Nature of Cultural Inte-
    gration and Change," in Edward A. Tiryakian (ed.). Sociological
    Theory, Values, and Sociocultural Change. London: Collier-Mac-
    millan Ltd., The Free Press of Glencoe, 1963.

Kluckhohn, Florence, and Strodtbeck, Fred L. Variations in Value Ori-
    entations. Evanston, Illinois: Row, Peterson and Co., 1961.

Knupfer, Genevieve. "Portrait of the Underdog," in Reinhard Bendix and
    Seymour Martin Lipset (eds.). Class, Status, and Power: A Reader
    in Social Stratification. Glencoe, Illinois: The Free Press of
    Glencoe, 1963.

Lasswell, Harold D., and Kaplan, Abraham. Power and Society: A Frame-
    work for Political Inquiry. New Haven: Yale University Press,
    1950.

Lemert, Edwin. Social Pathology: A Systematic Approach to the Theory
    of Sociopathic Behavior. New York: McGraw-Hill Book Co., Inc.,
    1951.

Lenski, Gerhard F., and Leggett, John C. "Caste, Class, and Deference
    in the Research Interview," American Journal of Sociology, LXV,
    No. 5 (March, 1960), 463-67.

Lipset, Seymour Martin. Political Man, The Social Basis of Politics.
    Garden City, New York: Doubleday and Co., Inc., 1960.

Litwak, Eugene. "Extended Kin Relations in An Industrial Democratic
    Society," in Ethel Shanas and Gordon F. Streib (eds.). Social
    Structure and the Family: Generational Relations. New Jersey:
    Prentice-Hall, Inc., 1965.

Litwak, Eugene. "Geographic Mobility and Extended Family Cohesion,"
    American Sociological Review, XXV (June, 1960) 385-94.

Litwak, Eugene. "Occupational Mobility and Extended Family Cohesion,"
    American Sociological Review, XXV (February, 1960) 9-21.

Loomis, Charles. Social Systems: Essays on Their Persistence and
    Change. Princeton, New Jersey: Van Nostrand Co., 1960.

Lynd, Robert S., and Lynd, Helen Merrell. Middletown, New York: Harcourt, Brace and Co., 1929.

Lynd, Robert S., and Lynd, Helen Merrell. _Middletown in Transition_. New York: Harcourt, Brace and Co., 1937.

Marx, Karl and Engels, Friedrich. _Manifesto of the Communist Party_. New York: International Publishers, 1922.

Mayer, Frederick. _Our Troubled Youth: Education Against Delinquency_. Washington, D. C.: Public Affairs Press, 1959.

Mead, Margaret. "The Contemporary American Family as an Anthropologist Sees It," in Herman D. Stein, and Richard A. Cloward (eds.). _Social Perspectives on Behavior_. Glencoe, Illinois: The Free Press, 1958.

Merton, Robert K. _Social Theory and Social Structure_. Revised and enlarged ed. Glencoe, Illinois: The Free Press, 1957.

Miller, S. M., and Riessman, Frank. "The Working Class Sub-culture: A New View," _Social Problems_, IX (Summer, 1961) 86-97.

Miller, Walter B. "Implications of Lower Class Cultures for Social Work," _The Social Service Review_, XXXIII (September, 1959) 219-36.

Miller, Walter B. "Lower Class Culture as a Generating Milieu of Gang Delinquency," _Journal of Social Issues_, XIV, No. 3 (1958), 5-19.

Mogey, J. M. _Family and Neighborhood_. Oxford: The Clarendon Press, 1956.

Newcomb, Theodore. _The Acquaintance Process_. New York: Holt, Rinehard and Winston, 1961.

Newcomb, Theodore M., Turner, Ralph H., and Converse, Philip E. _Social Psychology: The Study of Human Interaction_. New York: Holt, Rinehart and Winston, Inc., 1965.

Parsons, Talcott. "A Revised Analytical Approach to the Theory of Social Stratification," in Reinhard Bendix and Seymour Martin Lipset (eds.). _Class, Status, and Power: A Reader in Social Stratification_. Glencoe, Illinois: The Free Press of Glencoe, 1963.

Parsons, Talcott. "The Kinship System of the Contemporary United States," in Herman D. Stein, and Richard A. Cloward (eds.). _Social Perspectives on Behavior_. Glencoe, Illinois: The Free Press, 1958.

Parsons, Talcott. "The Social Structure of the Family," in Ruth N. Ashen (ed.). _The Family: Its Function and Destiny_. New York: Harper and Bros., 1949.

Parsons, Talcott, and Bales, Robert F. _Family, Socialization and Interaction Process_. Glencoe, Illinois: The Free Press, 1955.

Pfautz, Harold W. "Near-Group Theory and Collective Behavior: A Critical Reformulation," _Social Problems_, IX (Fall, 1961) 167-74.

Pitkin, Donald. "Land Tenure and Farm Organization in an Italian Village." Unpublished Ph.D. Dissertation, Harvard University, 1954.

Rainwater, Lee, Coleman, Richard P., and Handel, Gerald. Workingman's Wife: Her Personality, World, and Life Style. New York: Oceana Publications, Inc., 1959.

Reissman, Leonard. Class in American Society. Glencoe, Illinois: The Free Press of Glencoe, 1959.

Rodman, Hyman. "On Understanding Lower Class Behavior," Social and Economic Studies, VIII (December, 1959), 441-50.

Rodman, Hyman. "The Lower-Class Value Stretch," Social Forces, XLII (December, 1963), 205-15.

Rosen, Bernard C. "Race, Ethnicity, and the Achievement Syndrome," American Sociological Review, XXIV (February, 1959), 47-60.

Rosen, Bernard C. "The Achievement Syndrome: A Psychocultural Dimension of Social Stratification," American Sociological Review, XXI (April, 1956) 203-11.

Rosow, Irving. "Intergenerational Relationships: Problems and Proposals," in Ethel Shanas and Gordon F. Streib (eds.). Social Structure and the Family: Generational Relations. New Jersey: Prentice-Hall, Inc., 1965.

Schermerhorn, Richard. These Our People. Boston: D. C. Heath and Co., 1949.

Schneider, Louis, and Lysgaard, Sverre. "The Deferred Gratification Pattern: A Preliminary Study," American Sociological Review, XVIII (April, 1953) 142-49.

Sewell, William H., Haller, Archie O., and Straus, Murray. "Social Status and Educational and Occupational Aspiration," American Sociological Review. XXII (February, 1957), 67-73.

Sharp, Harry and Axelrod, Moris. "Mutual Aid Among Relatives in an Urban Population," in Ronald Freedman, et. al. Principles of Sociology. rev. ed. New York: Henry Holt and Co., 1956.

Short, James F., and Strodtbeck, Fred L. Group Process and Gang Delinquency. Chicago: The University of Chicago Press, 1965.

Simmel, Georg. "The Number of Members as Determining the Sociological Form of the Group," American Journal of Sociology, VIII (July, 1902), 1-46; and 158-96.

Simpson, Richard. "A Modification of the Functional Theory of Stratification," Social Forces, XXXV (December, 1956) 369-75.

Slater, P. E. "Contrasting Correlates of Group Size," Sociometry, XXI, No. 2 (June, 1958) 129-96.

Smith, Raymond T. The Negro Family in British Guiana: Family Structure and Social Status in the Villages. London: Routledge and

Kegan Paul, 1956.

Spergel, Irving. Racketville, Slumtown, Haulburg: An Exploratory Study of Delinquent Subcultures. Chicago: University of Chicago Press, 1964.

Srole, Leo. "Social Integration and Certain Corollaries: An Exploratory Study," American Sociological Review, XXI (March, 1960), 709-16.

Straus, Murray A. "Deferred Gratification, Social Class, and the Achievement Syndrome," American Sociological Review, XXVII (June, 1962), 326-35.

Strodtbeck, Fred L. "Family Interaction, Values, and Achievement," in D. C. McClelland, A. Baldwin, U. Bronfenbrenner, and F. Strodtbeck Talent and Society. Princeton, New Jersey: D. Van Nostrand, 1958.

Sussman, Marvin. "The Help Pattern in the Middle Class Family," American Sociological Review, XVIII (February, 1953) 22-28.

Sussman, Marvin. "The Isolated Nuclear Family: Fact or Fiction," Social Problems, VI (Spring, 1959) 333-40.

Sussman, Marvin and Buchinal, Lee. "Kin Family Network: Unheralded Structure in Current Conceptualizations of Family Functioning," Marriage and Family Living, XXIV (August, 1962) 231-40.

Sutherland, Edwin H., and Cressey, Donald R. Principles of Criminology. 6th ed. revised. New York: J. B. Lippincott Co., 1960.

Svalastoga, Kaare. "Social Differentiation," in Robert E. L. Faris (ed.). Handbook of Modern Sociology. Chicago: Rand McNally and Co., 1964.

Thibaut, John W., and Kelly, Harold H. The Social Psychology of Groups. New York: John Wiley and Sons, Inc., 1959.

Thomas, Edwin J. "Theory and Research on the Small Group: Selected Themes and Problems," in Leonard S. Kogan (ed.). Social Science Theory and Social Work Research. New York: National Association of Social Workers, 1959.

Thrasher, Frederic M. The Gang: A Study of 1,313 Gangs in Chicago. Chicago: The University of Chicago Press, 1927.

Thrasher, Frederic M. "The Gang," in A. Paul Hare, Edgar F. Borgatta, and Robert F. Bales (eds.). Small Groups: Studies in Social Interaction. New York: Alfred A. Knopf, 1961.

Tumin, Melvin. "Some Principles of Stratification: A Critical Analysis," American Sociological Review, XVIII (August, 1953), 387-94.

Tumin, Melvin. "Some Unapplauded Consequences of Social Mobility in a Mass Society," Social Forces, XXXVI (October, 1957) 32-37.

Warner, W. Lloyd and Lunt, Paul S. The Social Life of a Modern Community. New Haven: Yale University Press, 1941.

Welfare Federation of Cleveland, "Patterns of Grouping Within the United Youth Program," A report prepared for the Subcommittee to Study the Needs of Emotionally Disturbed Delinquent Adolescents. Cleveland, Ohio: Welfare Federation of Cleveland, 1959. (Mimeographed)

West, James. Plainville, U.S.A. New York: Columbia University Press, 1945.

Whyte, William F. Street Corner Society: The Social Structure of an Italian Slum. 2d ed. revised. Chicago: University of Chicago Press, 1955.

Wirth, Louis, "Urbanism as a Way of Life," American Journal of Sociology, XLIV (July, 1938) 1-24.

Wolff, Kurt H. (trans. and ed.). The Sociology of Georg Simmel. Glencoe, Illinois: The Free Press, 1950.

Woods, Frances J. The American Family System. New York: Harper and Brothers Publishers, 1959.

Wrong, Dennis W. "The Functional Theory of Stratification: Some Neglected Considerations." American Sociological Review, XXIV (December, 1959), 772-82.

Yablonsky, Lewis. "The Delinquent Gang as a Near Group," Social Problems, VII (Fall, 1959), 108-17.

Yablonsky, Lewis. The Violent Gang. Baltimore, Maryland: Penguin Books, 1966.

Young, Michael and Willmott, Peter. Family and Kinship in East London. London: Routledge and Kegan Paul, 1957.

Zelditch Jr., Morris. "Family, Marriage and Kinship," in Robert E. L. Faris (ed.). Handbook of Modern Sociology. Chicago: Rand McNally and Co., 1964.